100 YEARS OF HUNTING

THE ULTIMATE TRIBUTE
TO OUR HUNTING HERITAGE

From the Editors of Voyageur Press

With stories, artwork, and photographs from
Zane Grey, Lynn Bogue Hunt, Ernest Hemingway,
Patrick F. McManus, Art Wolfe, Edmund Osthaus, Archibald
Rutledge, Robert Ruark, Gordon MacQuarrie, Havilah
Babcock, William W. Headrick, Gustave Muss-Arnolt,
Jimmy Carter, John Madson, and more

Voyageur Press

Book designed by Andrea Rud
Jacket designed by Kristy Tucker
Printed in Hong Kong

99   00   01   02   03   5   4   3   2   1

Library of Congress Cataloging-in-Publication Data
100 years of hunting : the ultimate tribute to our hunting heritage / from the editors of Voyageur Press.
    p.   cm.
  ISBN 0-89658-414-3 (alk. paper)
  1. Hunting. 2. Hunting stories. I. Voyageur Press. II. Title: One hundred years of hunting.
SK33.A125   1999
799.2—dc21   99-22665
                    CIP

Distributed in Canada by Raincoast Books, 8680 Cambie Street, Vancouver, B.C. V6P 6M9

Published by Voyageur Press, Inc.
123 North Second Street, P.O. Box 338, Stillwater, MN 55082 U.S.A.
651-430-2210, fax 651-430-2211

Educators, fundraisers, premium and gift buyers, publicists, and marketing managers: Looking for creative products and new sales ideas? Voyageur Press books are available at special discounts when purchased in quantities, and special editions can be created to your specifications. For details contact the marketing department at 800-888-9653.

ON THE FRONTISPIECE, CLOCKWISE FROM TOP LEFT: *A beautiful collection of decoys. Owner: Ron Adamson. (Photograph © Howard Lambert); Early Velvet-Tikchik, Alaska (1993) by Bob White. (Courtesy of the artist); Canada goose hunting along the Missouri River in South Dakota. (Photograph © Mark Kayser); Hunting boot ad, 1922.*

PAGES 2–3, MAIN PHOTO: *A chukar hunter and his dog along Hell's Canyon, Snake River, Idaho. (Photograph © William H. Mullins)*

PAGE 3, INSET: *A content hunter and his dogs. (Photograph courtesy Pennsylvania State Archives, Record Group 31, Department of Commerce, Vacation and Travel Bureau)*

PAGE 5: *A hunter and his moose, northern Yukon, Canada, circa 1925. (Photograph courtesy Yukon Archives)*

CONTENTS

INTRODUCTION

THE HUNTING TRADITION

The twentieth century has been a revolutionary whirl-wind. No previous century contained such massive change for human society, technology, and the natural world. From the horse and buggy to the interstate highway system to the information superhighway, from Victorian-age morals to the free-form social mores of the late 1900s, from a predomi-nately rural society to a society of urbanites, those that have lived in the twentieth century have had to adapt to the chang-ing times.

MAIN PHOTO: *A huge flock of mallards in New Mexico. (Photograph ©
Art Wolfe)*

INSET: *Herter's Decoy ad, 1946.*

In many respects, the pursuit of game has been no different. In 1900, the vast majority of hunters sought their quarry close to home, usually within walking distance. In 2000, it is possible to be working in Boston on Friday and be hunting in the Montana Rockies on Saturday. Around the turn of the century, smokeless powder and telescopic sights were in their infancy, and repeating rifles were beginning to find wider use. Today, the technological options available to hunters is truly staggering—high-powered rifles, electronic tracking equipment, ATVs, Gore-Tex clothing, and so much more.

The game themselves have also fundamentally changed. In the first twenty years of the 1900s, at the close of the age of unregulated market hunting, the populations of bison, whitetailed deer, elk, pronghorn, wild turkey, and other animals reached low points. Many former game species—such as the passenger pigeon and the heath hen—had even been hunted to extinction by this time. At the end of the twentieth century, populations of most game animals have increased severalfold, including the whitetailed deer herd, which numbered 300,000 in 1920 and totals an estimated 27 million today.

Though all of this is certainly true and has undeniably changed the way we hunt, that is not what this book is about. This book is about tradition. For the vast majority of the 17 million North Americans who go afield in pursuit of game as the new millennium begins, a hunt is about such things as a connection to the land, bonding with a parent or child or friend, watching the instinct of a bird dog radiate outward from her rigid point, and treating game with the greatest respect. The core of the hunt, the very reasons that people go afield, is the same today as it was in 1900. Tradition.

A Brief History of Hunting in the Twentieth Century

In the outdoor realm, the twentieth century has been about conservation of game, and hunters led the way toward enactment of laws and changes in practices that allowed the hunting tradition to continue.

Before the turn of the century, there were few game laws at all to inhibit hunters. Truly stunning numbers of animals were killed, including 15,000 ducks a day on Chesapeake Bay, 10 million passenger pigeons a year in the Midwest alone, and some 4,200 bison within a year and a half by just one man, Buffalo Bill Cody.

Even before 1900, it became apparent to some that humans were putting wildlife in grave peril. Yellowstone National Park was formed in 1872 primarily as a wildlife refuge for bison. Toward the end of the nineteenth century, wealthy sportsmen and sporting organizations began to act in response to dwindling game supplies. Theodore Roosevelt and George Bird Grinnell, among others, founded the Boone & Crockett Club in 1887, not only "to promote manly sport with rifle," but also to encourage the observance of a sporting code for hunters. The code included such things as not taking more game than can be consumed by the hunter, not pursuing any game species to the point of extinction, having proper skill with weapons to deliver a humane coup de grâce in the field, and to allow prey a fair opportunity to escape (the concept of "fair chase"). In addition to sporting groups, the outdoors magazines, such as *Field & Stream* and *Outdoor Life*, took up the charge, promoting the hunters' code and pushing for legislation to end the unregulated shooting of game.

The new century brought results for these efforts almost immediately. The Lacey Act of 1900 prohibited interstate commerce in feathers and skins, effectively outlawing most forms of market hunting. A year later, Theodore Roosevelt himself became president of the United States. Though TR did not oversee the passing of significant regulations regarding hunting, the avid sportsman did lead by example, following the hunters' code in his days afield.

The federal government moved again in 1913, passing the Migratory Birds Law, which gave responsibility to the U.S. Department of Agriculture to fix seasons for the hunting of migratory birds and outlined penalties for violations of the law. In 1916, the Migratory Bird Treaty was signed with Great Britain (acting on behalf of Canada), extending similar provisions internationally for the first time. The U.S. government also authorized states to enact laws based on the federal statute, including bag limits, bans on the sale of migratory birds, and other important measures.

Duck hunters and retriever in an Alabama marsh at sunrise. (Photograph © Byron Jorjorian)

The Barr Lake Rod & Gun Club, Barr Lake, Colorado, 1910. (Photograph courtesy the Denver Public Library, Western History Collection)

Of course, more was needed if the hunting tradition was to survive. Newly formed conservation groups such as the National Audubon Society, the Izaak Walton League, and others took up the fight for preserving game—as well as non-game—species. One group took the concept a step further: Ducks Unlimited not only sought to preserve wildlife but to manage game in order to increase the population of game animals (waterfowl, in DU's case). Ducks Unlimited was founded in 1937, though their game management ideas dated back a quarter century.

The U.S. government continued to pass regulations to preserve game animals and habitats. The 1929 Migratory Bird Conservation Act authorized the purchase of land for waterfowl refuges. The Migratory Bird Hunting Stamp Act of 1934 established a federal waterfowl hunting licensing program and provided that proceeds from purchasing the stamp licenses would be used to buy refuges. Today, the federal government uses most of the $14 million collected annually under this law for habitat protection and law enforcement. Similarly, the Pittman-Robertson Act of 1937 established a tax on hunting equipment and ammunition, with the money to be used for game conservation.

Introductions of game also played a role in the development of hunting in the United States. One of the most-celebrated relative newcomers is the ringnecked pheasant, normally a resident of China. The pheasant was introduced in Oregon in 1881 and was first hunted in the 1890s. The well-known pheasant range of the Dakotas and Nebraska didn't have large populations of the birds until the 1920s. Similarly, Chukar partridge were introduced from India, eventually thriving in Nevada and Washington. Other game, such as elk and mule deer, were relocated within the United States; this is why today there are mule deer in Hawaii and elk in Minnesota.

What is the result of all of this? Quite frankly, these regulations made it possible for a hunting tradition to survive in North America. At the time the Migratory Bird Hunting Stamp Act was passed, many thought that duck and goose shooting was at an end. When deer populations hit their low point around 1900, few sportsmen thought deer could recover. It would be a different world for hunters if there were no deer to hunt, no waterfowl to pursue, no pheasants to flush. The laws of the twentieth century, the policies of sporting organizations, the writing in the sporting magazines, and the active introduction and reintroduction of game saved the hunting tradition in America.

ABOUT *100 YEARS OF HUNTING*

Tradition is what this book is about. The outdoors writers of the twentieth century speak here in a variety of voices about this tradition: Some are poetic, some are documentary, some are gripping, and some are

A brace of pheasants and a Browning Citori 20-gauge over-under shotgun. (Photograph © Ron Spomer)

introspective. But all provide a record of the times in which they lived, and, directly or indirectly, write fondly of the special connection to the land and to the game that drives humankind to hunt.

The writers in *100 Years of Hunting* include two former presidents of the United States, two winners of the Pulitzer Prize, one winner of the Nobel Prize, one of the most popular novelists of the twentieth century, several beloved outdoors writers made famous in the pages of *Field & Stream*, *Sports Afield*, and *Outdoor Life*, a Minnesota naturalist, a man who later in life became a successful fruit and vegetable farmer, and a geologist. It's really quite a mix.

The challenge of choosing selections for a book like this lies in the inevitability of not being able to use some important voices. For fans of the work of prominent outdoors writers such as Jack O'Connor, Corey Ford, Rick Bass, Thomas McGuane, Aldo Leopold, Theodore Roosevelt, and others worthy of inclusion, we sincerely apologize.

Of course, this isn't an anthology of words alone, but an illustrated collection that we hope will bring this century of hunting to life. We hope you will find this selection of color photographs, historical images, paintings, and vintage advertisements as remarkable and appealing as we do.

Today actual days afield are greatly limited. But the experience rests in your soul year-round, waiting patiently for the season opener. Until those hallowed autumn days begin anew, we hope this collection will help feed your yearning for the hunt.

The ultimate hunting accessory, 1933.

"Just Look at Them!" (1904) by Edmund Osthaus. (Courtesy the Hagley Museum and Library)

Successful elk hunters packing out their game. (Photograph © Alan and Sandy Carey)

100 YEARS OF HUNTING

As children, most of us learned to hunt. As adults, we go afield to recreate a little piece of that youthful enthusiasm. Our purpose is clear; our passion is strong; our excitement is high. We are traveling through time and becoming children again, free from the hassles and worries of adulthood, pursuing game in the wild lands of this vast continent. We are at peace, pursuing a time-honored tradition that has become, quite simply, a part of who we are.

It's time to begin. Let Edwyn Sandys carry you back, all the way to the turn of the century. Other voices will follow to move you forward in time, snapshots from the hunting tradition of twentieth-century North America.

MAIN PHOTO: *Fanned ruffed grouse tailfeathers with shell belt and game bag. (Photograph © Bill Marchel)*

INSET: *Hunting camp on Johnson's Ford, Gasconade River, Missouri, 1900. (Photograph courtesy the State Historical Society of Missouri, Columbia)*

A RED=LETTER DAY

By Edwyn Sandys

Edwyn Sandys was born in Canada, where he served as editor to *Canadian Sportsman* and worked as a journalist for Canadian Pacific Railways. Later in his career, he relocated to New York to become editor of *Outing*. He also contributed numerous articles to other leading magazines of the day.

The author of four books about hunting and game animals—*Upland Game Birds* (1902), *Trapper Jim* (1903), *Sportsman Joe* (1904), and *Shooting Sketches* (1905)—Sandys wrote extensively about his outdoors experiences. He died in 1909.

Dr. Frank Cheatham Wilson and his dogs, circa 1900. (Photograph courtesy the Georgia Historical Society)

THE SUN LOOMS large above a sea of gauzy haze which piles like airy surf against the forest's rim. It is a windless, dreamy morning, rich with the magic of the Indian summer, the glory of painted leaves, the incense of ripe fruit. In the full fatness of autumn's latter days the world is songless, silent, fat. Those things which sleep—that drowse the long, white silence soon to be—are round well-nigh to bursting. Those things that durst not face the nip of steel-skied nights have fled to kindlier climes, while those other things which neither sleep nor flee are revelling in a rich abundance. They know what must come when Kee-way-din whines about their brushy eaves and the strange, cold white feathers fall. They know that the brushy and still leafy cover will be flattened and that the white wolf of the North will plunge and ramp and howl across far leagues of whiteness. They know the present business of their kind is to eat—eat till craws and skins are tight as drumheads, to wax fat because fat things do not freeze, while they can, if need be, doze for days when times are bad. All this eating and fat content is lazy business and sleep lasts long.

Up in the pleasant room, too, Sleep herself sits by a narrow cot upon which lies a silent figure. The kindly goddess knows that under her spell men do no wrong, and so, with light hand laid across his eyes, she sits and watches. Through open windows streams a scented air, fruity from near-by orchards and spiced with the breath of drying foliage.

Thump! A big apple parts its failing stem and strikes a hollow roof. The figure stirs and Sleep flies on soundless feet. Gradually the man gets himself dressed and then he looks the workman. The loose cord breeches closely match the broad-soled, flat-heeled knee-boots; the sweater has the shade of the dried grass, and the old canvas coat admirably matches it. 'Tis a marvel, that coat—a thing of beauty and a joy forever to its owner—a horror unspeakable to his female kin. One had described it as 'A snarl of pockets held together by some remnants of filthy canvas,' and the owner had merely smiled. To him every stain upon it was a precious thing, a sign-board pointing to a dear-prized memory, and he wouldn't trade it for the mantle of Elijah. Once, a fair young thing, a frequent guest, who was clever at giving the last touch to ties and an invaluable adviser in regard

to manicure sets, had declared she'd 'wash that horrid jacket!' and thus a glimmering possibility of a—a—oh! bother—it didn't come off, anyhow!

But the little woman who met him this morning was not of that sort. Once, long before, he had explained to her the difference between shooting for count and shooting as a sportsman should, and why there was no advantage in getting upon Bob White ground too early. She knew that fifteen birds was his limit so far as that particular game was concerned, and she also knew that the fifteen and perhaps some other game would load that coat at night, if all went well. So when he had nearly finished breakfast, she slipped away, to presently return amid a tumult of scratching claws and gusty breathing.

'Here—he—is—and—I—gave—him—just—three—bits!' she panted, as the strong brute strained at the chain in his eagerness.

'Down—you!' muttered the man, and as the quivering form sank promptly, he continued—'Mater mine, thou fibbest—he don't lick his chops that way after straight bread.'

'Merely an atom of gravy, dear—just a drop was kept, and the bread is so dry and he chews at it so.'

'Grease—faugh! will you never learn?' he growls, but his eyes are twinkling and he has to avert his face to keep from laughing outright, for this question of dog-fare is a rock upon which they regularly split. Right well he knows that Don has had his bread, a trifle of meat, and perhaps about a pint of soupy stuff to boot; but he wisely makes no further comment, for the mistake was lovingly made.

And so they fare forth, a varmint-looking team, both lean and hard, the long, easy stride of the man hinting of many days afoot, the corky action of the dog proving him sound and keen. 'Tis true his ribs show as though his hide covered a spiral spring, but his white coat has a satiny lustre, and he puts his feet down as though such things as thorns and burrs had never been. Behind them stands the little figure watching with moist eyes, for one is hers and the other belongs to one of hers. Though they went and returned one thousand times in safety,—still—still—it might—be. Wonderful are thy ways, O woman!

At the corner the tall figure halts and right-

A 1928 A. H. Fox 20-gauge "CE" grade shotgun. (Photograph © William W. Headrick)

about-faces with military precision, the gun is whipped through the salute, and at the instant the white dog rises erect upon his hind feet. Both man and dog know that all these things must be done before rounding the turn, else the day would not be all it should. A kerchief flutters in the distance, then they pass in a few strides from town to country.

Before them spreads a huge pasture, beyond that a grove of mighty trees, and beyond that the shooting grounds—farm after farm, with here a bit of woods and there a thicket. For miles the country is the same, and through it all, in a bee-line, extends the double track of an important railway. Along either side of this runs a broad ditch, now bone-dry and bordered with low catbriers. These and the ripe weeds standing thickly in the angles of the rail-fences form rare good cover for scattered birds.

'Well, Mister,' says the man to the dog, 'guess you'd better have a pipe-opener right here.' He waves his hand and clucks softly, and the dog sails away over the short

ABOVE: *The northern bobwhite quail, South Texas. (Photograph © Michael H. Francis)*

RIGHT: *An English pointer on a staunch point. (Photograph © Bill Buckley/The Green Agency)*

fall grass. A judge of dogs would watch this pointer with solid satisfaction. So smooth is his action and so systematic is his method of covering ground, that his tremendous speed is not at first apparent. But for all that he is a flier which few dogs can stay with, and best of all he can keep going for a week if need be.

Of course, he naturally was a fine animal, blessed with courage and brains a plenty, but his owner's method—'keep sending 'em,' as he termed it—has done much to develop the speed. Needless to say, at the for-ward end of that dog is a nose—for woe unto the animal that would attempt such a clip without the very finest thing in the way of a smeller.

Half an hour later the man halts on top of a fence while the dog takes a roll. They are now on the edge of the good ground, and both feel just right after their preliminary canter. The man fills his pipe, gets it nicely going, then looks at the gun across his knees. It appears almost like a toy; but its small tubes are of the best and can throw lead with amazing power. Almost plain, but

perfect of its pattern, that gun cost about three times what an unsophisticated person might guess as its price, and, as its owner declared, it was well worth the money.

'Now, Mister,' says the man, after a bit, 'there's rag-weed, standing corn, and thicket—which would you advise?' The dog sits up and stares with loving intentness, and the man continues—'When a lemon-headed fool-dog looks at me after that manner he certainly means standing corn, so here goes.' At the words he lets himself down, while the dog darts away. Soon he is into his regular stride and beating the ground with beautiful precision. The man watches and nods his head as he mutters, 'That rat-tailed rascal's going great guns to-day, he'll have 'em befo——' In the middle of a stride the dog has halted as though smitten by lightning. Some message of the air has reached that marvellous nose, and the grand brute stands as though carved in marble. There was no roading, no feeling for it, just an instantaneous propping and a breathless halt. 'That's funny,' mutters the man; 'I'd have sworn—ha!' There is an abrupt rising of a brown, hasty-winged thing which goes darting for a distant cover. At the sight the lazy man suddenly changes. The little gun leaps to the level, and before the butt has fairly touched the shoulder, the quick smokeless has hurled its leaden greeting. The bird goes down, unmistakably clean killed, while the dog slowly sinks to his haunches. As the man reloads, his face fairly shines with joy. 'Fifty yards if an inch,' he says to himself, 'and a bruising old hen at that. Who'd have expected a woodcock this time of year and away out here?' Then he goes to the dog and clucks him on.

As the dog has seen the bird fall, he merely makes a few bounds forward and again stiffens within two yards of an unusually large female woodcock—one of those choice birds only occasionally picked up at the tail-end of the season. 'Don't like that, eh?' laughs the man as he holds the bird near the dog's nose. The grand eyes are bulging with controlled excitement, but the shapely muzzle is wrinkled into an expression highly suggestive of disgust. 'Wish I understood that. It's funny, but you don't like a dead cock though you'll stop on 'em fast enough when alive—eh, old boy?' chuckles the man. 'Here, take it,' he says, and the dog obeys. 'Give it to me,' continues the man, and the dog promptly drops the bird into the hand, then wrinkles his chops as though an unpleasant flavor remained. It's a grand

bird, old and fat, and the druggist's scales later prove it to weigh a full eight ounces, an extreme weight for even a female, which is larger than the male.

When again started, the dog sweeps away to a low-lying bit where the withered corn is taller and thicker. Here he circles rapidly, stops for a moment, then stands looking at his master. The man moves over to him, and closely examining the ground presently detects half-a-dozen small hollows and a tiny brown feather. 'Flushed, eh?' he says to the dog, and evidently the latter agrees. Now the man's own tracks show plainly, there are no other bootmarks, nor has he seen an empty shell anywhere; so he knows the flush has been owing to natural cause. 'Mebbe hawk,' he says to himself. 'If so, where?' His eyes rove over all the surrounding cover and settle upon a clump of thicket in a corner. It is about far enough and certainly looks promising. Away goes the dog as though he could read the other's thoughts. As he nears the edge of the cover his style changes. The smooth gallop slows to a steady trot which presently alters to a majestic march. Higher and higher rises the square muzzle and up and up and up goes the tapering stern, while he steps ahead as though treading on tacks. Two yards from the cover he halts with lifted foot in the perfection of the old-fashioned stylish point. 'You beauty!' says the man, his eyes flashing with delight. Then he goes to the wonderful white form which, hard from set muscles, yet quivers with the tenseness of sudden excitement. The man, too, feels the magic of the situation. His eyes gleam and his teeth grip the pipe-stem as if they would shear it off. His heart thrills with rapturous anticipation and his strong hands grip the gun ready for instant action. Right well he knows that the pointer never draws like that or raises head and stern so high except for serious business. A dead leaf falls ticking through the tangling twigs, and at the first move of it the dog gives a convulsive twitch, while the gun flashes to the level and down again. A smile flickers in the keen eyes as the man moves a step nearer. No matter which way the game may go, he is bound to have a fair chance and he knows it. The cover is none too thick for even a straight-away drive, while all other directions mean the broad open. He clucks softly to the dog, but there is no responsive move—clearly this is a serious case. Could it possibly be a——? Ah! the roar of him, as he tore like a feathered shell through the densest growth! Oh! the beauty of him, as he curved into the mellow sunshine, his dainty crest and plumes flattened with speed. And, ho! the smashing thump of him as he hit the ground some thirty yards away. 'Twas a brave dash, Sir Ruffs, but risky withal, to dare that sunny open in defiance of trained eyes and nervously quick hands. Was it yonder mat of new clover-tips, or the red fruit of the briar-rose, which coaxed you here a fourth of a mile from your woodland stronghold?

But the dog is eager to be off. The languid air, scarce drifting in its lazy mood, is tattling something. There is some unfinished business, which the strong scent of the expected grouse had interrupted. Now, as the dog slants away, the square muzzle rises higher, and the eager stern whips frantically. Shorter and shorter grow the tacks, until the advance steadies to a straight line. Soon the gallop slows to a canter, a trot, a stately walk. With head and stern held high, on he marches until fifty yards have been covered. Then he suddenly stiffens, while the quivering nostrils search the air for positive proof. His erstwhile gusty breathing is muffled now, his jaws slowly open and close, while the marvellous nose seems to be feeling—feeling for a something rarely pleasant. Then on again, slower and slower, till he seems to fairly drift to his anchorage. Then his hindquarters sink till he is almost on his hams.

Has he got them? Man, if you'd ever followed that dog, you'd know he had 'em. When you see that long draw and the squatting finish, bet your gun, or your wife, or whatever you prize most, that it's a bevy and a big one. Scattered birds he will pin in all sorts of fancy attitudes as he happens upon them, but when he gets right down to it, that signifies a wholesale order. The man moves up within a foot of the stiffened stern. For a moment the tenseness is dramatic—then—whur-r-r! Something like a mighty shell loaded with feathered baseballs appears to explode in a patch of dried grasses, and the air is filled with humming missiles. Even in the roar and electric rush the trained eyes mark slight differences in coloration, and the trim tubes swing from one bird to a second with a smooth rapidity which betokens years of practice. Two birds fall a few yards apart, and as they turn over in the air, the man notes the flash of white and knows his lightning choice has been correct. As he moves toward them, there is a sudden hollow roar, and a lone bird rises from his very foot and goes whizzing toward cover. The gun leaps to shoulder before he can check it, but it is promptly low-

ered. 'Go on, you old seed-hen, and do your best next year,' he chuckles, as the brown matron strives to set herself afire by atmospheric friction. Her course is wide of that taken by the brood, but he knows she'll call the stragglers to her ere the shadows fall.

And they will be stragglers. Of the twenty strong beauties that roared up ahead of that first point, her sweet, insistent 'Ca-loi-ee! ca-loi-ee!' will muster but four when fence and thicket blur together in the scented dusk. Instead of doing as she had told them time and time again—instead of plunging headlong into the convenient woods, her headstrong family has whirred across the open and dropped here and there in the well-known resort, the railroad ditch. Hither they have come day after day until the awful, clattering trains have lost all terrors. In the broad ditch are pleasant runways and much useful gravel of assorted sizes, also cosey, sunny spots, the perfection of dust baths. Here, too, are many unaccountable stores of grain, choicest of corn and wheat, which seem in some miraculous manner to appear there all ready for eating. What better place could there be?

The man looks at the dog and grins with unholy joy. The dog looks at the man and seems to understand. Oh! they are a precious pair of rascals, are these two.

'You old Judas,' says the man, 'we'll do things to 'em now. It looks like fifteen straight—eh?'

And the dog cuts a couple of fool-capers, which is his method of evincing a devilish approval. Then the pair of 'em move on after the misguided birds.

Whur! Bing! Whur! Bing! It is almost too easy. Shooting in that ditch where cover is barely knee-high with a high embankment on one side and a stiff fence on the other, is something like shooting into an enormous funnel—the shot has to go right. The dog does little more than trot from point to point. Bird after bird rises and is cut down with painless exactitude. Presently two start together, only to be dropped by a quick double-hail. Then one curves over the fence, but a rising mist of downy feathers tells that he got it just in time. Then another pair, and as the second barrel sounds, a third rises. The cases leap from the gun, a hand flashes to and from a pocket—Burr!

'Here's where we quit—that makes fifteen,' says the man as the last bird is gathered. He sits down on a convenient knoll, pushes his hat back, and grins at the dog. That worthy, after a hesitating forward movement, which would indicate his belief that 'There's more,' also sits down and stares expectantly at the grimy coat. 'Yes, I'll give you half. You've done mighty well, and for once it's fifteen straight,' chuckles the man as he produces the sandwiches. The dog gets a bit more than half, for this is a red-letter day. Then the pipe comes out, and for half an hour the pair of 'em lounge in perfect peace. Little do they know or care about trouble. Twin tramps are they, heedless of the burdens of life, careless of its future. Sufficient for them that the afternoon sun is warm, the grass thick and dry. Naught care they for the five-mile homeward trudge, for neither is more than comfortably tired, and when they rise refreshed they will stride away as though they had just begun.

And the little woman will have two glorious meals all ready, for she knows what each can do in that line when thoroughly in earnest. And she will be almost sinfully happy, for the first glance will tell that things have gone well for at least one November day.

Remington Shur Shot Shell ad.

After the Storm–Quail Shooting *(1989) by Bob White. (Courtesy of the artist)*

LYNN
BOGUE
HUNT

QUAIL SHOOTING

By Grover Cleveland

Stephen Grover Cleveland was the only man in American history to serve two non-consecutive terms as president of the United States. He was elected to his first term in 1884 while serving as governor of New York, despite being dogged by scandal during the campaign: Rumors circulated widely that the bachelor Cleveland had fathered an illegitimate child. But he won nonetheless—the first Democrat to rise to the White House after the Civil War—only to lose the Presidency in 1888 to Benjamin Harrison. Cleveland returned in 1892, however, defeating Harrison and regaining the White House for four more years.

Cleveland was an avid outdoorsman, spending a good amount of free time—particularly after his retirement from public service—hunting and fishing. In addition to such "presidential" books as *Principles and Purposes of Our Form of Government* (1892) and *Presidential Problems* (1904), Cleveland authored *Fishing and Shooting Sketches* (1906), from which "Quail Shooting" is taken.

Bobwhite Covey *(1916) by Lynn Bogue Hunt.*

WE HEAR A great deal in these days about abundant physical exercise as a necessary factor in the maintenance of sound health and vigor. This is so universally and persistently enjoined upon us by those whose studies and efforts are devoted to our bodily welfare that frequently, if we withhold an iota of belief concerning any detail of the proposition, we subject ourselves to the accusation of recklessly discrediting the laws of health.

While beyond all doubt a wholesale denial of the importance of physical exertion to a desirable condition of bodily strength would savor of foolish hardihood, we are by no means obliged to concede that mere activity of muscles without accompaniment constitutes the exercise best calculated to do us good. In point of fact we are only boldly honest and sincere when we insist that really beneficial exercise consists as much in the pursuit of some independent object we desire to reach or gain by physical exertion, coupled with a pleasant stimulation of mental interest and recreation, as in any given kind or degree of mere muscular activity. Bodily movement alone, undertaken from a sense of duty or upon medical advice, is among the dreary and unsatisfying things of life. It may cultivate or increase animal strength and endurance, but it is apt at the same time to weaken and distort the disposition and temper. The medicine is not only distasteful, but fails in efficacy unless it is mingled with the agreeable and healing ingredients of mental recreation and desirable objects of endeavor.

I am convinced that nothing meets all the requirements of rational, healthful outdoor exercise more completely than quail shooting. It seems to be so compounded of wholesome things that it reaches, with vitalizing effect, every point of mental or physical enervation. Under the prohibitions of the law, or the restraints of sporting decency, or both, it is permitted only at a season of the year when nature freely dispenses, to those who submit to her treatment, the potent tonic of cool and bracing air and the invigorating influences of fields and trees and sky, no longer vexed by summer heat. It invites early rising; and as a general rule a successful search for these uncertain birds involves long miles of travel on foot. Obviously this sport furnishes an abundance of muscular action and physically strengthening surroundings. These, fortunately, are supplemented by the eager alertness essential to the discovery and capture of game well worth the effort, and by the recreative and self-satisfying complacency of more or less skillful shooting.

In addition to all this, the quail shooter has on his excursions a companion, who not only promotes his success, but whose manner of contributing to it is a constant source of delight. I am not speaking of human companionship, which frequently mars pleasure by insistent competition or awkward interference, but of the companionship of a faithful, devoted helper, never discouraged or discontented with his allotted service, except when the man behind the gun shoots badly, and always dumbly willing to concede to the shooter the entire credit of a successful hunt. The work in the field of a well-trained dog is of itself an exhibition abundantly worth the fatigue of a quailing expedition. It behooves the hunter, however, to remember that the dog is in the field for business, and that no amount of sentimental admiration of his performances on the part of his master will compensate him, if, after he has found and indicated the location of the game, it escapes through inattention or bad shooting at the critical instant. The careless or bungling shooter who repeatedly misses all manner of fair shots, must not be surprised if, in utter disgust, his dog companion sulkily ceases effort, or even wholly abandons the field, leaving the chagrined and disappointed hunter to return home alone—leg weary, gameless and ashamed. He is thus forced to learn that hunting-dog intelligence is not limited to abject subservience; and he thus gains a new appreciation of the fact that the better his dog, the better the shooter must know "what to do with his gun."

I do not assume to be competent to give instruction in quail shooting. I miss too often to undertake such a *rôle*. It may not, however, be entirely unprofitable to mention a fault which I suppose to be somewhat common among those who have not reached the point of satisfactory skill, and which my experience has taught me will stand in the way of success as long as it remains uncorrected. I refer to the instinctive and difficultly controlled impulse to shoot too quickly when

Pre-1913 L. C. Smith A-2 grade 20-gauge ejector gun. (Photograph © William W. Headrick)

the bird rises. The flight seems to be much more speedy than it really is; and the undrilled shooter, if he has any idea in his mind at all, is dominated by the fear that if the formality of aiming his gun is observed the game will be beyond range before he shoots. This leads to a nervous, flustered pointing of the gun in the direction of the bird's flight, and its discharge at such close range that the load of shot hardly separates in the intervening distance. Nine times out of ten the result is, of course, a complete miss; and if the bird should at any time under these conditions be accidentally hit, it would be difficult to find its scattered fragments. An old quail shooter once advised a younger one afflicted with this sort of quick triggeritis: "When the bird gets up, if you chew tobacco spit over your shoulder before you shoot."

It is absolutely certain that he who aspires to do good quail shooting must keep cool; and it is just as certain that he must trust the carrying qualities of his gun as well as his own ability and the intelligence of his dog. If he observes these rules, experience and practice will do the rest.

I hope I may be allowed to suggest that both those who appreciate the table qualities of the toothsome quail, and those who know the keen enjoyment and health-giving results of their pursuit, should recognize it as quite worth their while, and as a matter of duty, to co-operate in every movement having for its object the protection, preservation and propagation of this game. Our quail have many natural enemies; they are often decimated by the severity of winter, and there are human beings so degraded and so lost to shame as to seek their destruction in ways most foul. A covey of quail will sometimes huddle as close together as possible in a circle, with their heads turned outward. I have heard of men who, discovering them in this situation, have fired upon them, killing every one at a single shot. There ought to be a law which would consign one guilty of this crime to prison for a comfortable term of years. A story is told of a man so stupidly unsportsman-like that when he was interfered with as he raised his gun, apparently to shoot a quail running on the ground, he exclaimed with irritation: "I did not intend to shoot until it had stopped running." This may be called innocent stupidity; but there is no place for such a man among sportsmen, and he is certainly out of place among quail.

It is cause for congratulation that so much has been

done for quail protection and preservation through the enactment of laws for that purpose. But neither these nor their perfunctory enforcement will be sufficiently effective. There must be, in addition, an active sentiment aroused in support of more advanced game legislation, and of willing, voluntary service in aid of its

enforcement; and in the meantime all belonging to the sporting fraternity should teach that genuine sportsmanship is based upon honor, generosity, obedience to law and a scrupulous willingness to perpetuate, for those who come after them, the recreation they themselves enjoy.

A hunter afield with his dogs near Phoenix, Arizona, 1906. (Photograph courtesy the Arizona Department of Library, Archives and Public Records, History and Archives Division, #97-8048)

ABOVE: *The Sportsman's Creed in a Federal Cartridge Corporation ad.*

FACING PAGE: Steady, Now . . . *(1914) by Gustave Muss-Arnolt. (Courtesy the Hagley Museum and Library)*

MOUNTAIN SHEEP IN THE OLD ROCKIES

By Daniel Moreau Barringer

Daniel Moreau Barringer was a passionate hunter, having been one of the original founders of the Boone & Crockett Club, and the inventor of two rifle sights that found wide use afield. But it was as a mining engineer and geologist that he is best known. In 1905, Barringer became the first to advance the theory that a forty-two-hundred-foot diameter crater in Arizona was created by the impact of a meteor with the earth, a rather radical idea in his day. Drilling operations proved him correct in 1920.

As a sportsman, Barringer knew that luck plays a role in just about any hunt. Sometimes luck is on the hunter's side; sometimes even the most experienced outdoorsman will find the deck stacked against him. "Mountain Sheep in the Old Rockies" is excerpted from the Boone & Crockett Club's *Hunting at High Altitudes*, edited by George Bird Grinnell.

The elusive Rocky Mountain bighorn. (Photograph © Dušan Smetana)

With my friends Charles Penrose and Granville Keller, and an exceedingly lazy and worthless boy, Frank, whom we hired to look after the horses, we were returning to Bozeman after about two months successful hunting among the headwaters of the Stinking Water and Upper Yellowstone Rivers. At the head of Sheep Creek, a small tributary, I think, of Trail Creek, we had turned off the direct route in order to spend our very last days of the hunt trying to get a good mountain sheep head. The time of the year was early November, and there were then plenty of sheep in this locality, for they had already come down from the higher mountains. Before this, I had had experience in hunting sheep, but up to that time I had not—nor have I yet—been successful in getting a very good head. I have grown to believe that, when it comes to hunting Rocky Mountain sheep, I am a Jonah, although it has been my good fortune to be quite successful in hunting other kinds of American big game.

One morning, the last of our hunt, I arose long before daybreak, prepared and ate a hurried breakfast and got well started by star-light. As has always been my custom when still-hunting, I went alone.

Before there was strong daylight I ran across a bunch of sheep, and I am ashamed to say that I fired at them, without knowing whether or not there was a good ram in the bunch. In the dim light I seemed to see a big sheep, and fired at it on the chance that it was a ram. I was gratified on going over to the spot at which I had seen the sheep, to find that I had made two clean misses, since their tracks showed that there were several ewes and lambs in the bunch. At the time I was using a splendid English Holland & Holland double express hammer rifle, .450 caliber, the shells being loaded with something like 120 grains of Curtis & Harvey black powder and heavy solid lead bullets, containing about 1-20 tin. I have always believed in plenty of lead, backed up by plenty of powder, and it is rather hard for me to become reconciled to the modern high power rifles. My experience with them at ranges over one hundred yards—that is after the bullet has settled down and is rotating steadily on its major axis—has not been as satisfactory as with the old-time ammunition. I am told that there are new and very effective methods, with which I am not familiar, of making the small bullet expand without splitting into several pieces, even after it has settled down and its rear end is not wobbling

about like a top before it "goes to sleep"—as we used to say when we were boys—which is supposed to be the cause of their making such terrible wounds at short ranges. If so, the modern rifles certainly have many and great advantages over those of the old style.

About sunrise I found myself a long way from camp, and an hour or so later saw in the distance a band of sheep lying down. With my glass I could see a fine ram among them. As the wind was wrong, I made a very long detour, and at the end of more than an hour found myself behind a rock, which I had long before selected as the point from which I would attempt a shot. Just as I was about to peer cautiously around the rock I felt the wind hit me in the back of the neck, and an instant later came the sound of scampering feet and all I could see as I ran around the rock was a sheep vanishing behind another big rock a hundred yards away.

Cursing my luck, but knowing that there was very little use in attempting to follow them, I wended my way toward another mountain, and as the sheep happened to be going my way, I more or less followed their trail, not with any hope of seeing them again but simply because their way was my way. Reaching the other mountain, I found myself in open pine and juniper timber, and to my great surprise soon noticed from the sign in the snow that the sheep had scattered; in fact, had commenced to feed. I of course devoted myself to the track of the big ram and proceeded as carefully as if walking on eggs.

I followed him for perhaps a quarter of a mile, the wind being right, and this time holding true. I finally noticed the track pass around a very large juniper tree, one of those large and dense junipers of Montana which many of us know so well and which would be so beautiful in our eastern parks, with a spread on the ground of densely foliaged limbs perhaps forty to fifty feet in diameter and tapering in a perfect cone to the highest branch in the middle. The ram's tracks were very fresh and as it was the only track to be seen in the newly fallen snow to the right or left for many yards, I entertained the hope that when I should get around the juniper I might catch a glimpse of him beyond it. So I carefully crept around the snow-covered bushy base of the tree, both barrels cocked, expecting every instant to get a shot. I continued to walk around the tree until I found myself on the side opposite that from which I

ABOVE: *A western hunting party, 1909. (Photograph courtesy the Oregon Historical Society, #76055-537)*

RIGHT: *Carbide Brilliant Search Light ad, 1921.*

had first started to go around it. The ram's track still kept ahead of me circling the juniper. I followed carefully. When I was three-quarters of the way around the tree I was amazed that I had not previously noticed his track on that side of it, which was to my left when I first commenced to go around it; but as he kept on I followed directly after him. Imagine my surprise and high disgust to find when I had completed the circuit of the tree that there was the ram's track in my own boot track. No sign of him anywhere; only the evidence of long jumps in the snow, for he had doubtless

started off at a run as soon as he got my scent. Yet I had not heard a sound. I then came to the conclusion that that particular ram was not for me, and with hopes still high, I proceeded to try to find another bunch of sheep.

About midday I ran across a mountain lion's track, practically as fresh as my own. Not having recently seen any sheep, and thinking that I might possibly get a glimpse of this lion, I followed him. He soon became aware of the fact, and proceeded to have some sport with me, for, as could be easily determined from the prints in the snow, he would wait for me to come in sight, and then would trot along a little further, get another point of observation, sit down and wait for me to reappear. The country was rough, and I did not think it wise to make the loops to leeward so necessary in still-hunting moose in the far north, to come upon the game from an unexpected direction. After following the lion for an hour or more, constantly expecting to see him before he could see me, and at a moment when, unfortunately, I was keeping my eyes glued on the snow trail ahead of me, I saw out of the corner of my eye a dun-colored body flash from a tree not more than forty yards distant. Before I could shoot it had disappeared among some rocks. I afterward found that this particularly provoking beast had been sitting on a low branch of a tree in full view all the time. Had I raised my eyes from the ground no doubt I would have had an excellent shot and would have had a good chance to add to my list of American big game one of the two kinds which I have never been privileged to kill; the other being a mountain goat.

Thinking that luck would change sooner or later I ate my meager lunch and made for camp over a country which I had not yet hunted. I found plenty of evidence of sheep but did not see one. Finally, however, in the late afternoon I came upon the track of the biggest sheep that I have ever trailed in my life and to my surprise and gratification I found that his track was about as fresh as my own. I started after this sheep and had not followed him a hundred yards before I saw him climbing the rocks ahead of me at a great pace. Before I could cock my rifle and shoot, he was almost on the sky line, about a hundred and twenty-five yards away. I am afraid that in my haste I saw rather too much

of the front sight and sent both bullets straight over his back. I supposed from his movements that he had already found me out and was trying to get away. Imagine my surprise, therefore, when as I was putting two new cartridges in my rifle, the ram reappeared on top of the hill and without a moment's hesitation returned full drive on his back trail. I gleefully said to myself, "Luck has changed at last," and so patiently and, as I thought, very coolly, waited for him to come nearer, meanwhile admiring and counting as my very own his magnificent head. On he came, and not until he was within ten or fifteen feet of me did I wave my rifle at him and yell. He reared on his hindlegs, the most startled sheep that it has ever been my good or bad fortune to see. I threw the rifle to my face and pulled and pulled

When the hunter is in bighorn country, the game holds a distinct advantage. (Photograph © Neal and M. J. Mishler)

and pulled. I know that I came very near pulling those two triggers off, and before I could realize what had happened, the ram made a lunge into the thick underbrush at one side and was gone. I had forgotten to cock either barrel!

I now made my way to camp as fast as I could leg it, with my hat brim well down over my eyes, determined to look neither to the right or to the left, for I had come to the conclusion that there was no use trying to buck against luck like that. I soon arrived at camp, and hardly waiting for dinner, crawled into my sleeping bag, like Job refusing to be confronted. The next day we broke camp and went on to Bozeman. I hope that that sheep is alive to this day—at least, that nobody else ever got him.

O Joy! Sleeping Bag ad, 1929.

Presidents Afield

In addition to Grover Cleveland and Jimmy Carter, whose writing about days afield appear in this book, other Chief Executives picked up their guns and summoned their dogs for outings in pursuit of game. Calvin Coolidge, president from 1923–1929, poses (below) with waterfowl from a hunting trip to Sapelo Island, Georgia, in 1928. Coolidge's predecessor, Warren Harding, also pursued game, as shown here (facing page, top photo) on a hunt in an image from the year of his death in office (Harding is on the right). Of course, Teddy Roosevelt, shown here (facing page, bottom photo) on a moose hunt in Quebec, Canada, in 1915, is renowned for his hunting exploits in North America and Africa. (Roosevelt photograph courtesy the Theodore Roosevelt Collection, Harvard College Library. Harding photograph courtesy the Library of Congress. Coolidge photograph courtesy the Georgia Department of Archives and History.)

GEESE

By Rex Beach

It has always been my failing," Rex Ellingwood Beach once wrote, "to quit the thing I am doing before it is well or completely done and try something new." Indeed, Beach studied law early on but quit to travel to the Klondike and participate in the gold rush of 1897. He spent five years in Alaska, and while there he had the chance to read the writings of Jack London, which inspired him to quit prospecting and write fiction about some of his own adventures in the north. He began to publish stories in the popular magazines of the turn of the century, and published his first book, *Pardners,* in 1905, a collection of stories about his Alaskan days. Some three dozen books and plays followed, many of which were made into motion pictures and all of which contributed to Beach's considerable wealth. Later in life, he changed gears yet again, and made another fortune growing flowers and vegetables.

"Geese" comes from his collection *Oh Shoot! Confessions of an Agitated Sportsman.*

A skyful of snow geese. (Photograph © Henry H. Holdsworth/Wild by Nature)

MOST MEN ENJOY hunting, or would if they had a chance, but there is a small, abnormal minority who are hopeless addicts to the chase. To them the fiscal year begins with the opening of the deer season or the start of the duck flight, and ends when "birds and quadrupeds may no longer be legally possessed." They are the fellows who wrap their own fish rods, join outing associations, and wear buckskin shirts when they disappear into the trackless wastes of Westchester County for the club's annual potlatch and big-game lying contests.

To this class I belong. I offer what follows not as an excuse, but as a plea in extenuation. It is a feeble effort to paint the optimistic soul of a sportsman, to show how impossible it is to prevent him from having a good time, no matter how his luck breaks, and, in a general way, to answer the question, "Why is a hunter?"

There is no satisfactory answer to that query; hunters are merely born that way. Something in their blood manifests itself in regular accord with the signs of the zodiac. In my case, for instance, when autumn brings the open season, I suffer a complete and baffling change of disposition. I am no longer the splendid, upright citizen whose Christian virtues are a joy to his neighbors and an inspiration to the youth of his community. No. I grow furtive and restless; honest toil irks me. I begin to chase sparrows and point meadow larks and bark at rabbit tracks. I fall ill and manifest alarming symptoms which demand change of climate and surcease from the grinding routine. I sigh and complain. I moan in my sleep and my appetite flags. I allow myself to be discovered dejectedly fondling a favorite fowling piece or staring, with the drooping eyes of a Saint Bernard, at some moth-eaten example of taxidermic atrocity. The only book that stirs my languid soul is that thrilling work, *Syllabus of the Fish and Game Regulations.*

So adept have I become at simulating the signs of overwork that seldom am I denied a hunting trip to save my tottering health. Mind you, I do not advocate deceit. I abhor hypocrisy in the home, and I merely recount my own method of procedure for the benefit of such fellow huntsmen as are married and may be in need of first aid.

I was suffering the ravages of suppressed desires, common to my kind, when, several autumns ago, a friend told me about a form of wild-goose shooting in vogue on the outer shoals of Pamlico Sound, North Carolina, and utterly stampeded my processes of orderly thought.

"They use rolling blinds on the sand bars," he told me. "They put down live decoys, a couple hundred yards away, then, when the geese come in, they roll the blind up to them."

I assured him that his story was interesting but absurd. Having hunted Canada honkers, I knew them to be suspicious birds, skeptical of the plainest circumstantial evidence and possessed of all the distrust of an income-tax examiner.

"You don't move while they're looking," my informant told me. "When they rubber, you hold your breath and, if religiously inclined, you pray. When they lower their heads, you push the blind forward. A goose is a poor judge of distance, and you can roll right up to him if you know how."

Peters Shells ad, 1921.

The fruits of a day afield. (Photograph courtesy the Oregon Historical Society, #91 9557-538)

I didn't believe him; but the next day I was en route to North Carolina, and I have been back there every year since. I have shot from rolling blinds, stake blinds, and batteries. Sometimes I have good luck, again I do not. But nothing destroys my enjoyment, and every trip is a success. Once I am away with a gun on my arm, I become a nomad, a Siwash; I return home only when my sense of guilt becomes unbearable and when the warmth of my wife's letters approaches zero.

And I have done well down there. At first, I went alone, traveled light, and spent little money. Now I take friends with me; I keep a well-equipped hunting boat there the year round; I stay a long time, and I spend sums vastly larger than I can afford. A brace of ducks used to cost me perhaps ten dollars, in the raw; now they stand me several times that, exclusive of general overhead. It shows what any persistent sportsman may accomplish even with a poor start. Perhaps no habitual hunter pays more for his entertainment than I do, and, figuring losses in business, time wasted, etc., etc., I truthfully can say that I enjoy the sport of kings.

This year there were five of us in the party— Maximilian Foster and Grantland Rice, fellow scribes, and Duke and Duchess, two English setters of breeding that we took along to investigate the quail resources of the country.

Max had made the trip once before; so he needed no urging to go again—only an excuse. We hit upon a good one. He is an abandoned trout fisherman and he ties his own flies. Feathers are expensive and hard to get. Why not lay in a good supply? It was the best we could think of at short notice; so he went home to try it out.

There was every reason why Grant should remain

at his desk, but we argued that there might well be problems of trajectory involved in goose shooting which would revolutionize the golf industry if thoughtfully studied. Who could better investigate this promising field than a recognized golf paranoiac like him? We had only to suggest this line of thought; Grant rose hungrily to the bait and darted with it into the uptown Subway. He argued where it would do the most good, and to such effect that he promised to follow us a week later.

Now, a word about Duke and Duchess. In my time I have owned many dogs, for a dog is something I lack the force of character to refuse. Anybody can give me any kind of dog at any time, and I am grateful—to the point of tears. That is how these two came to our house—as gift dogs—and they made me very happy for a while, because I had always wanted a pair of setters. Frankly, however, they abused their welcome, for there has seldom been merely a pair of them. I have presented setter puppies to my relatives and to my friends. I am now preparing a gift list of my business acquaintances and fellow club members, but I am slowly losing ground, and my place grows more and more to resemble a Bide-a-Wee Home.

I had never been able to hunt over this pair, for whenever I was ready for a trip, household duties prevented Duchess from going along, or else I foresaw the necessity of taking with me a large crate in which to ship back her excess profits. This time, however, conditions appeared to be propitious, so Max and I decided to do upland shooting while waiting for Grant to join us, and then wind up our hunt with a gigantic offensive against the ducks and geese. After watching Duke and Duchess point some of my pigeons and retrieve corncobs, Max and I decided they were natural game sleuths and could detect a bird in almost any disguise. If a quail hoped to escape them, it would have to wear hip boots and a beard.

Time was, not long ago, when travel was no great hardship. But all that is changed. Government operation of the railroads worked wonders, even during the brief time we had it. For instance, it restored all the thrill and suspense, all the old exciting uncertainty of travel during the Civil War wood-burning days. No longer does one encounter on the part of employees that un-American servility which made travel so popu-

lar with the parasitic rich. Real democracy prevails; train crews are rough, gruff, and unmannerly, and even the lowly porter has learned the sovereign dignity of labor—and maintains it. Nor is there now any difference in the accommodations on the jerkwater feeders and the main lines, all that having yielded to the glorious leveling process. Train schedules are ingeniously arranged for the benefit of innkeepers at junction points, and the last named are maintained for the purpose of allowing one train to escape before another can interfere with it.

Having missed connections wherever practical, and taken the dogs out for a walk in several towns of which we had never heard, Max and I arrived, in due course, at Beaufort, only twelve hours late. We were a bit weak from hunger and considerably bruised from futile attempts to battle our way into the dining car, but otherwise we were little the worse for the journey.

The guides were waiting with the boat, but they bore bad news.

"There's plenty of geese on the banks," Ri told us, "but we've had summer weather and the tides are so low there's no shooting."

Seldom does a hunter make a long trip and encounter weather or game conditions that are anything except unparalleled. I have learned long since to anticipate the announcement that all would have been well had I arrived three weeks earlier or had I postponed my coming for a similar length of time; therefore we ignored Ri's evil tidings, pointed to Duke and Duchess, and forecast a bad week for any quail that were unwise enough to remain in the county.

Both Ri and Nathan are banks men, born and raised close to the Hatteras surf; they know nothing of quail hunting, so we blueprinted it for them on the way to the dock.

"High-schooled dogs like these are almost human," we explained. "They are trained to pay no attention to anything except game birds, but, with respect to them, their intelligence is uncanny, their instinct unerring. They will quarter a field on the run, pick up the scent of a covey, wheel and work up wind to a point. When they come to a stand, you know you've got quail. You walk up, give them the word to flush; then they retrieve the dead birds and lay them at your feet without marring a feather. It's beautiful work."

A pair of English setters on point. (Photograph © Mark Kayser)

While we were in the midst of this tribute, Duke, whose leash I had removed, squeezed out through the picket fence of a back yard with the palpitating remains of a white pullet in his mouth. He was proud; he was atremble with the ardor of the chase; the irate owner of the deceased fowl was at his heels, brandishing a hoe.

I settled with the outraged citizen; then I engaged Duke in a tug of war for the *corpus delicti*. It was a strictly fresh pullet; there was nothing cold storage about it, for it stretched. Meanwhile, Max explained how to break a dog of chicken-stealing.

"Tie the dead bird round his neck where he can't get at it. That will cure him."

"But why cure him?" Ri inquired, earnestly. "Seems like you'd ought to encourage a habit of that kind. Them dogs is worth *money*!"

Duke and Duchess were much interested in the boat. While we unpacked, they explored it from end to end; then Duchess went out on deck, tried to point a school of mullet, and fell overboard. Nathan retrieved her with a boat hook; she came streaming into the cabin, shook herself thoroughly over my open steamer trunk, then, unobserved, climbed into my berth and pulled the covers up around her chin. She has a long, silky, expensive coat, and it dries slowly; but she liked my bed and spent most of a restless night trying to blot herself upon my chest.

I did not sleep well. No one can enjoy unbroken repose so long as a wet dog insists upon sleeping inside the bosom of his pajamas. I arose at dawn with a hollow cough and all the premonitory symptoms of pneumonia, but Duchess appeared to be none the worse for her wetting, and we felt a great relief. It would have

A matched pair of Purdey side-by-side shotguns, built in 1904. Owner: Jack Publisi's Gun Emporium. (Photograph © Howard Lambert)

been a sad interruption to our outing had either dog fallen ill.

That day, while the boat was being outfitted, Max and I hired an automobile and went out to start a rolling barrage against the quail. The dogs were shivering with excitement when we put them into the first field, but they had nothing on us, for few thrills exceed that of the hunter who, after a year indoors, slips a pair of shells into his gun and says, "Let's go."

But within a half hour we knew we had pulled a flivver. Out of the entire state of North Carolina we had selected the one section where big, inch-long cockleburs were too thick for dogs to work. Nothing less than a patent-leather dachshund could have lived in those fields. In no time Duke and Duchess were burred up so solidly they could hardly move. They were bleeding; their spun-silk coats were matted and rolled until their skins were as tight as drum heads; their plumy tails were like baseball bats, and they weighed so much that their knees buckled and they looked as if they were about to jump.

They put up a covey or two, but it became a question either of removing their coats in solid blankets, as a whale is stripped of its blubber, or of patiently freeing them, one burr at a time—an all-day task—so we went back to the car and sought a snipe marsh.

Snipe marshes are wet, and the mud is usually deep, dark, and sticky. One either stands or sits in it, and to get the fullest enjoyment from the sport one should forget his rubber boots. This we had done; hence we were pretty squashy when we got back into the automobile about dark. We slowly froze on the way to town, but before we had hoarsed up too badly to speak, we agreed that it had been a great day.

I picked burrs most of that night. Along toward morning, however, I realized that it was a hopeless task. I had hair all over the cabin; my fingers were bleeding, Duke and Duchess were upon the verge of hysteria, and whenever we looked at each other we showed our teeth and growled. So I decided to clip them. But it is no part of a vacation to shear a pair of fretful canines, size six and seven-eighths, with a pair of dull manicure scissors. Breakfast found those dogs looking as if they had on tights. I was haggard, but grimly determined to enjoy another day in the glorious open if only I could stay awake.

It was no use trying to hunt here, however; so I gave the word to up anchor and hie away out of the cocklebur belt.

So far as I can discover, a boat owner has one privilege, expensive but gratifying; he can, when the spirit moves him, say, "Let us go away from here," and sometimes the boat goes. I voiced that lordly order, ran Duchess out of my bed, and lay down for a nap. But not to sleep. Ri and Nathan began an intricate and noisy job of steam fitting in the engine room. Now and then the motor joined them, only to miss, cough, and die in their arms. By and by I heard echoes of profanity; so I arose to investigate the nature of the difficulty.

Max was frowning at the engine; Ri was massaging its forehead with a handful of waste; Nathan was spasmodically wrenching hisses out of it with the starting bar. He raised a streaming face to say:

"She never balked on us before."

Ri agreed:

"She never missed an explosion coming over."

"Sure you've got gas?" I hopefully inquired. This is my first question in cases of engine trouble.

They were sure; so I returned to my bunk and ran Duchess out of my warm place. Had they answered my inquiry in the negative, I could have instantly diagnosed the case, but when an engine has gasoline and still refuses to run, I delve no deeper. I respect its wishes.

Another half hour passed; then I went forward and asked if there was plenty of spark. This is my second question, and it leaves me clean. But there was spark enough, so I effaced myself once for all and again disturbed Duchess just as she had made an igloo of my bedclothes. This time I dozed off, lulled by sounds which indicated that Nathan had begun a major operation of some sort, with the others passing instruments and counting sponges.

Running footsteps roused me. Max was removing a fire extinguisher from its rack when I opened my eyes. He was calm; nothing to worry about except a small conflagration under the engine-room floor. If we worked fast, we might save a part of the ship, and wasn't it fortunate that we were still tied up to the dock?

Contrary to expectations, we managed to put out the blaze, after which we found that all our motor needed was a cozy little fire in its living room to take

Canada geese. (Photograph © Richard Hamilton Smith)

the chill out of the air, for when we turned it over it went to work in the most cheerful spirit.

That afternoon we hunted farther up the sound, but what quail we raised were in impossible thickets and the snipe on the marshes had gone visiting over the week end. As we pulled out at daybreak on the following morning, we ran aground on a falling tide and stuck there.

Some trips seem to have a jinx on them. John W. Jonah appears to keep step right up to the finish. After laboring long and blasphemously in a vain effort to get afloat, the unwelcome suspicion entered our minds that this was such a one.

I had built this boat especially for hunting in these shallow waters, and while she is not much to look at, she is warm and comfortable, and it is Ri's boast that she is the only fifty-foot craft in existence that can navigate on a heavy frost or a light dew. But that is an exaggeration, as we discovered when, finally, we were forced to go overboard, regardless of the weather, and boost her off by main strength. Then we learned that she had been cunningly designed to draw just enough water so as to thoroughly wet us, regardless of the height of our waders. But the experience benefited our colds; it did them a world of good and practically renewed their youth.

Max and I tested out the game resources of several sections of that shore on the way to Ocracoke, but instead of shipping quail home to our expectant friends, we had hard work to get enough to keep body and soul together, and those few, of course, we could neither taste nor smell—our colds were doing so well. Always there was some good reason why we had shot nothing to-day but had high hopes for the morrow; Duke and Duchess began to regard the whole expedition as a hoax on them, and spent their time collecting ticks for me to remove during the evening. Nevertheless, the open life was having its effect upon Max and me. We had arrived soft, pallid, gas-bleached, our bones afflicted with city-bred aches and pains; after a week spent on waist-deep sand bars, in damp marshes and draughty fields, we were practically bedridden.

Ocracoke, center of the goose-hunting industry, is a quaint New England village pitched on the outer rim of Pamlico Sound, and it hovers around a tiny circular lagoon. The houses are scattered among wind-twisted cedars or thickets of juniper and sedge, and most of them possess two outstanding adjuncts—a private graveyard and a decoy pen. All male inhabitants above the age of nine are experts on internal-combustion engines, for motor boats are everywhere except in the back yards. Of distinctive landmarks there are four—one lighthouse, one colored man, and two Methodist churches. Ocracoke has tried other negroes, but likes this one, and as for religion, it will probably build another Methodist church when prices get back to normal.

Now, for the benefit of any reader genuinely in quest of information, a word as to the kind of hunting here in vogue and the methods involved. First, understand that this stormy Hatteras region is the Palm Beach of the Canada goose and his little cousin the brant. Ducks winter all along the Atlantic coast, but Pamlico Sound marks, roughly, the goose's southern limit. Here each wary old gander pilots his family; here he and his mate watch their young folks make social engagements for the following season.

Woolrich out-of-doors sportswear ad, 1929.

ABOVE: *Sign from the long-disbanded Sisters Island Hunting Club in southern Illinois. (Photograph © William W. Headrick)*

RIGHT: *Snow geese at dawn. (Photograph © Tom Walker)*

There is no marsh or pond shooting, for the wild fowl frequent the shallow waters of the sound and it is necessary to hunt from rolling blinds, stake blinds, or batteries. The rolling blind I have described—it is used only on cold, drizzly days in the late season when the geese have chilblains and gather on the dry bars to compare frost bites. A stake blind resembles a pulpit raised upon four posts, and is useful mainly in decoying inexperienced Northern hunters. Green sportsmen stool well to stake blinds, for they are comfortable, but a wise gunner shies at them as does a gander. He knows that the real thing is a battery.

This latter device may be described as a sort of coffin, but lacking in the creature comforts of a casket. It is a narrow, water-tight box with a flush deck about two feet wide, to three sides of which are hinged large folding wings of cloth or sacking stretched upon a light wooden framework. It is painted an inconspicuous color; heavy weights sink it so low that its decks are awash. The sportsman lies at full length in it, and his body is thus really beneath the level of the water. When it is surrounded by a couple hundred dancing decoys, the hunter is effectually hidden from all but high-flying birds. To such as fly low, the rig is a snare and a delusion; not unless they flare high enough to get a duck's-eye view do they see the ace-in-the-hole, and then it is usually too late.

Battery shooting requires some little practice and experience. One must begin by learning to endure patiently the sensations of ossification, for to rest one's aching frame even briefly by sitting up, or to so much as raise one's head for a good look about, is a high crime and a misdemeanor. It completely ruins the whole day for the guides, who are comfortably anchored off to leeward in the tender, and affords them the opportunity of saying, later:

"You can't expect 'em to decoy to a lump. If you'd of kep' down, you'd of got fifty birds to-day."

And that is not the only discomfort. All batteries are too small, and some of them leak in the small of the

A trio of gunners swing their shotguns skyward at passing snow geese. (Photograph © Bill Marchel)

back. If the wind shifts or blows up, they sink before the guides arrive. For years I tried to adapt myself to the existing models, but failed. I fasted until my hips narrowed to an AA last; I wore the hair off the top of my head; my body became rectangular, and still I did not fit. I have had rubber-booted guides stand upon my abdomen and stamp me into my mold, as the barefoot maidens of Italy tread the autumn vintage, but, no matter how well they wedged me in, some part of me, sooner or later, slipped. The damp salt air swelled me, perhaps; anyhow, I bulged until from a distance I looked like a dead porpoise, and the ducks avoided me.

Tiring of this, I had a large box built. I equipped it with a rubber mattress and pillow, and now I shoot in Oriental luxury. But, even under favorable conditions, to correctly time incoming birds, to rise up and "meet them" at precisely the right instant, is a matter of considerable nicety. One must shoot sitting, which is a trick in itself, especially on the back hand, and ducks do not remain stationary when surprised by the apparition of a magnified jack-in-the-box. They are reputed to travel at ninety miles an hour, when hitting on all four, but that is too conservative. Start the goose flesh on a teal's neck, for instance, and he will leave your vicinity so fast that a load of shot needs short pants and running shoes to overtake him.

I have lain in a double box alongside of experienced field shots and picked up many valuable additions to my vocabulary of epithets. I have seen nice, well-bred, Christian gentlemen grind their teeth, throw their shells overboard, and send for better loads, even smash their guns in profane and impotent rage. That is, I have seen them perform thus when I myself was not stone blind with fury.

We shot for a couple of days, off Ocracoke, while we were waiting for Grant, but the weather was warm and we had little luck; then the bottom fell out of the glass and, in high hopes of a norther, we ran up the banks to our favorite hunting grounds. As we pulled into our anchorage, the bars were black with wild fowl; through our field glasses we could see thousands, tens of thousands, of resting geese; up toward Hatteras Inlet the sky was smudged with smoky streamers which we knew to be wheeling clouds of redheads. Before we had been at rest a half hour, the wind hauled and came whooping out of the north, bearing a cold, driving rain; so we shook hands all around. All that is necessary

for good shooting on Pamlico is bad weather. It looked as if we had buried our jinx once for all.

Our party had grown, for we had picked up the hunting rigs at Ocracoke—they were moored astern of us, launches, battery boats, and decoy skiffs streaming out like the tail of a comet. All that day and the next we watched low-flying strings of geese and ragged flocks of ducks beating past us, while we told stories or conducted simple experiments in probability and chance. In the latter I was unsuccessful, as usual, for I simply cannot become accustomed to the high cost of two small pair.

The second morning brought a slight betterment of conditions; so we set out early, Max in search of shelter behind a marshy islet, while I hit for the outer reefs. After several attempts, Ri finally found a spot where a mile of shoals had flattened the sea sufficiently to promise some hope of "getting down."

While we were placing the battery, Grantland Rice arrived in a small boat from Ocracoke. He was drenched; he had been four days en route from New York, and he was about fed up on rough travel. Through numb, blue lips he chattered, "You're harder to find than Stanley."

I directed him to the houseboat and told him where to obtain comfort and warmth—third bureau drawer, left-hand corner, but be sure to cork it up when through—then explained that Max had put down a double box and was waiting for him.

"The weather to kill geese is weather to kill men," I assured him. "You're in luck to arrive during a norther like this."

"Any nursing facilities aboard the boat?" Grant wanted to know.

I assured him with pride that we were equipped to take care of almost anything up to double pneumonia, and that if worse came to worst and his lungs filled up, we could run him over to the mainland, where he could probably get in touch with a hospital by mail.

My battery managed to live, with the lead wash strips turned up, but the gale drove foam and spray over me in such quantities that I was soon numb and wet—the normal state for a battery hunter. Members of the Greely expedition doubtless suffered some discomforts, and the retreat from Serbia must have been trying, but for 100-per-cent-perfect exposure give me a battery in stormy winter weather.

However, I managed to collect a fair number of

Winchester Model 12 shotgun, Herter's goose decoy, and other memorabilia. Owners: Jim Meyer and Rich Lowe. (Photograph © Howard Lambert)

birds before dusk, when, in answer to my feeble signals, the guides rescued me. They seized me by my brittle ears, raised me stiffly to my heels, then slid me, head first, into the tiny cabin of the launch, as stokers shove cordwood into a boiler. By the time we got back to the boat I could bend my larger joints slightly and I no longer gave off a metallic sound when things fell on me.

The other boys had not fared so well. They had been drowned out, their battery had been sunk without trace, and they had nothing to show for their day's sport except a clothes line full of steaming garments and a nice pair of congestive chills. Otherwise it had been a great day, and we looked forward to more fun on the morrow.

But how vain our hopes! As usual, the weather was

unparalleled. Once again it surprised the oldest inhabitants. That night the wind whipped into the south, drove all the water off the bars, then fell away to a calm, and the temperature became oppressive. The wild fowl reassembled in great rafts where we could not get at them; we lay in our batteries, panting like lizards and moaning for iced lemonade, while the skin on our noses curled up like dried paint. The only birds we got were poor half-witted things, delirious with the heat.

Such conditions could not last—the guides assured us of that—and they didn't. The next day it rained, and a battery in rainy weather is about as dry as a goldfish globe. Now, a strong man with an iron will may school himself to lie motionless while he slowly perishes from cold, for after the first few agonizing hours there is comparatively little discomfort to death by freezing, but I defy anybody to drown without a struggle.

But why drag out the painful details? We had not interred our jinx. One day a hurricane blew out of the north and piled the angry waters in upon us, the next it shifted, ran the tides out, and left us as dry as a lime burner's boot; the third it rained or fogged or turned glassy calm. Grizzled old veterans from the Hatteras Life-saving Station rowed out to tell us that such weather was impossible and threatened to ruin their business, but what could you expect under a Democratic administration?

One morning, Ri outlined a desperate plan to me, and I leaped at it. Away inshore, across miles of flats, we could see probably a million geese and twice that many ducks enjoying a shallow footbath where no boat could approach them.

"Let's leave the launch outside, wade our rig up to their feedin' ground, and dig it in. It'll take a half day of hard work, but there's goin' to be a loose goose flyin' about three o'clock, and you can shoot till plumb dark. We'll leave the box down and wade back."

It sounded difficult, so we tried it, towing the empty battery behind us. The big decoy skiff dragged like an alligator, but we poled, waded, shoved, and tugged until we came to where the bottom was pitted and white with uptorn grass roots. Here we dug a hole deep enough to sink the box—no easy job with a broken-handled shovel—put out our stools, and then the men shoved the empty boat away.

Tons of wild fowl had gone out as we came in, but soon after I lay down they began returning. First there came a pair of sprigs, then a pair of black ducks. The black mallard is my favorite—he is so wary, so wise, and so game. He can look into the neck of a jug, and he fights to the last. When the hen dropped, the drake, as usual, flared vertically. Upward he leaped in that exhibition of furious aerial gymnastics peculiar to his breed; then, at the top of his climb, he seemed to hang motionless for the briefest interval. That is the psychological instant at which to nail a black duck. As he came down, fighting, I was up and overboard after him. The water was shallow, but I splashed like a stern-wheeler, and I was wet to the waist before I had retrieved that cripple.

Next I glimpsed a long, low line of waving wings approaching, and flattened myself to the thickness of a flannel cake, thrilling in every nerve. Never did twenty geese head in more prettily. They had started to set their pinions, and I was picking my shots, when one of the decoys, a young gander in the Boy Scout class, cracked under the nervous strain and began to flap madly. He flared the incomers, and I failed to get more than two.

I made haste to gather up the dead birds and lay them on the battery wings; then I moved the shell-shocked gander to the head of the rig. But before I could get him anchored, distant honks warned me, and I ran for cover. Of course, I tripped over decoy lines—everybody does. I did Miss Kellerman's famous standing, sitting, standing dive, but there was still a dry spot between my shoulder blades when I plunged kicking into the battery. I was too late, however, and the flock went by, out of range, laughing uproariously at me.

Then up from the south came a rain squall, and I stood with my back to it, shivering and talking loudly as tiny glacial streams explored parts of my body that are not accustomed to water. During the rest of the afternoon, cloudbursts followed one another with such regularity that my battery resembled a horse trough, and when I immersed myself in it it overflowed. But between squalls the birds flew. When a bunch of geese pitched in at my head and I downed five, I fell in love with the spot and would have resisted a writ of eviction.

When the guides appeared at dark I had a pile of game that all but filled the tiny skiff which they had thoughtfully brought along. By the time we had loaded it with the dead birds and the crate of live decoys it was gunwale deep, so we set out to wade back to the launch, towing it behind us.

Night had fallen; fog and rain occasionally obscured the gleam of our distant ship's lantern. Other lights winked at us out of the gloom, and although they were miles away, nevertheless they all looked alike; so, naturally, we got lost. We headed for first one then another twinkling beacon, and altered our course only when the water deepened so that we could proceed no farther without swimming.

I have been successfully lost where you would least expect it, but never before had I been lost at sea with nothing whatever to sit down upon except the ocean, and after an hour or two I voted it the last word in nothing to do. I can think of no poorer way of spending a rainy December night than chasing will-o'-the-wisps round a knee-deep mud flat the size of Texas, with an open channel between you and the shore.

I presume we waded no more than twenty-five miles—although it seemed much farther—before we found the launch and collapsed over her gunwale like three wet shirts. Then, just to show that things are never as bad as possible, the engine balked.

I asked if there was plenty of gas and if the spark was working, and, receiving the usual affirmative answer, I dissolved completely into my rubber boots. Ri was probably quite as miserable as I, but he began to scrub up for the customary operation. He removed the motor's appendix, or its Fay and Bowen, and ran a straw through it, the while we could see frantic flashes of the houseboat's headlight.

I felt an aching pity for Max and Grant. What a shock to them it would be to find us in the morning, frozen over the disemboweled remains of our engine, like merrymakers stricken at a feast of toadstools. They were men of fine feelings; it would nearly, if not quite, spoil their whole trip, even though they divided my dead birds between them.

But the machine made a miraculous recovery, and at its first encouraging "put" a great warmth of satisfaction stole through me. After all, it had been a wonderful day.

Human endurance, however, could not out-game that weather. The evening finally came when the boys announced that their time was up, so, after supper, we sent the small boats up to Ocracoke on the inside and fared forth into the dark sound.

As we blindly felt our way out from our anchorage, we ran over a stake net, picked it up and wrapped it around our propeller, and grounded helplessly on the edge of the outer bar. There we stuck. Examination showed a very pretty state of affairs. The net with its hard cotton lead line had wedged in between the propeller and the hull, and disconnected the shaft—a trifling damage and one that could have been repaired easily enough had we possessed a deep-sea diving outfit or a floating dry dock. But, search our baggage as we might, we could find neither. That's the trouble about leaving home in a hurry, one is apt to forget his dry dock.

The familiar V-formation of Canada geese in flight. (Photograph © Richard Hamilton Smith)

Just to show us that he was still on the job, old J. W. Jinx arranged a shift in the wind. It had been calm all day; now a gale came off the sound and held us firmly on the reef. Pamlico began to show her teeth in the gloom, and with every swell we worked higher up on the bar and the boat bumped until our teeth rattled. We were several miles offshore, without any sort of skiff; it began to look as if we had about run out of luck and might have to hunt standing room somewhere in the surf. However, a yacht had made in near by on the day before, and, thanks to our searchlight, we managed to get a rise out of her. She sent a launch off, and it finally towed us back to shelter.

By this time it was midnight and the duties of host rested heavily upon me. I could with difficulty meet the accusing eyes of my guests, and, although I had exhausted my conversational powers, I hung close to them for fear of the cutting, unkind things they would say if I left them alone.

The next morning, Mr. Scott, owner of the neighboring yacht, prompted by true sportsman's courtesy, towed us back to Ocracoke, and as we went plunging down the sound in a cloud of spray we realized that the weather had hardened up and the birds were beginning to fly. The sky was full of them; we could hear the noise of many guns—a sound that brought scalding tears to our eyes.

I simply could not bear to leave just as the show had begun; so I reread my wife's last letter, and, finding it only moderately cool, I took the bit in my teeth and declared it my intention to stick long enough to change defeat into victory, even if I had to sleep in the woodshed when I got home.

"Better stay on for a few days," I urged the boys. "It will be dangerous to sit up in a battery to-morrow; the birds will knock your hats off. A blind man could kill his limit in this weather."

I had not read their mail, but I understood when they choked up and spoke tearfully about "business." While I pitied them sincerely, a fierce joy surged through my own veins; nothing now could hinder me from enjoying a few days of fast, furious shooting. The birds were pouring out of Currituck; there would be redheads, canvasbacks, teal—every kind of duck.

As we tried to work the house boat into the lagoon at Ocracoke, where we could get her out on the ways and count the fish remaining in that fragment of net, an Arctic tornado hit us and blew us up high and dry on a rock pile. It was a frightful position we now found ourselves in, for we had such a list to port that the chips rolled off the table and we all felt lucky.

But the storm had delayed the mail boat and my companions were forced to remain over another day. The courage with which they bore this bitter disappointment was sublime; they sang like a pair of thrushes as they feverishly unpacked.

Conditions were ideal the next morning and we were away early. Having put down my rig in shallow water, where I could wade up my own birds, I sent the launch back to the village. This promised to be a day of days, and I wanted to get the most out of it.

Almost immediately the ducks began flying, and several bunches headed in towards me. I was puzzled as to why they changed their minds and flared, until a cautious peep over the side showed a small power-boat threshing up against the wind. It had already cost me several good shots, but there was nothing to do except wait patiently for it to pass. However, it did not pass; in spite of my angry shouts and gesticulations it held its course until within hailing distance. Then the man in the stern bellowed:

"Telegram!"

Now, mail is bad enough on a hunting trip, but telegrams are unbearable, and I distrust them. Nobody ever wanted me to stay away and enjoy myself so urgently as to wire me; therefore I openly resented this man and his mission. By the time he had handed me

No birds get through *his* shot patterns

An advertisement sketch for Winchester shells from the Missouri Ruralist, *1919. (Courtesy the State Historical Society of Missouri, Columbia)*

ABOVE: *Oregon goose hunters in the early twentieth century. (Photograph courtesy the Oregon Historical Society, #58924-537)*

LEFT: *Goose hunter poses with his game after a day afield along the Missouri River, 1929. (Photograph courtesy the Historical Society of Missouri, Columbia)*

The popularity of the automobile brought with it a need for accessories to accommodate the needs of sportsmen. Both the 1922 Chenango Camp Trailer and the 1929 Bird Dog Palace provided comfort for hunters and canines alike.

the message I had made up my mind to ignore it, reasoning rapidly that it could by no possibility be of importance, and if it were—as it probably was—I could do nothing about it before the mail boat came that night. Hence it was futile to permit my attention to be distracted from the important business of the moment.

I thanked the man, then urged him, for Heaven's sake, to beat it quickly, for, in the offing, flocks of geese were noisily demanding a chance to sit down with my decoys, and just out of range ducks were flying about, first on one wing then on the other, waiting for him to be gone.

But that telegram exercised an uncanny fascination for me. I lacked the moral courage to destroy it, although I knew full well if I kept it on my person I would read it—and regret so doing. Things worked out just as I had expected. I yielded and—my worst apprehensions were realized. The message was from my wife, but beyond that fact there was nothing in its favor, for it read:

Your secretary has forged a number of your checks and disappeared. Total amount unknown, as checks are still coming in. Presume you gave him keys to wine cellar, for they, too, are missing. Wire instructions quick. Am ill, but stay, have a good time, and don't worry.

I stared, numb and horror-stricken, at the sheet until I was roused by a mighty whir of rushing pinions. Those ducks had stood it as long as possible and were decoying to me, sitting up. Through force of habit my palsied fingers clutched at my gun, but, although the birds were back-pedaling almost within reach, I scored five misses. Who can shoot straight with amount of loss unknown and certain precincts unheard from? Not I. Those broadbills looked like fluttering bank books.

And the keys to the wine cellar missing! That precious private stock, laid in for purely medicinal purposes, ravaged, kidnaped! A hoarse shout burst from my throat; I leaped to my feet and waved frantically at the departing boatsman, but he mistook my cries of anguish for jubilation at the results of my broadside, waved me good luck, and continued on his way.

As I stood there striving to make my distress heard by that vanishing messenger, geese, brant, ducks, and other shy feathered creatures of the wild poured out of the sky and tried to alight upon me, or so it seemed.

They came in clouds and I shooed them off like mosquitoes. One would have thought it was the nesting season, and I was an egg.

I read again that hideous message as I undertook to reload, but I trembled the trigger off and barely missed destroying my left foot—my favorite. Never in the annals of battery shooting has there been another day like that. Those ducks reorganized and launched attack after attack upon me, but my nerve was gone, and the most I could do was defend myself blindly.

I did spill blood during one assault, and I was encouraged until I found that I had shot one of Ri's live decoys. Beyond that, the casualties were negligible, and when the guides came to pick me up they had to beat the blackheads out of the decoys with an oar.

As we pulled out of Ocracoke at dawn the next morning, the town was full of dead birds, and visiting sportsmen with eager, feverish eyes were setting forth once more for the gunning grounds. But we hated them. Flocks of geese decoyed to the mail boat whenever it hove to or broke down, and we hated them also.

Upon my arrival home I found a wire from Ri reading:

> Too bad you left. Nathan killed fifty birds the next day and he can't hit a bull with a spade.

However, take it by and large, it was a fine trip and a good time was had by all, which proves what I set out to demonstrate in the beginning—*viz.*, you can't explain a hunter; you can only bear with him and allow nature to take its course.

Goose hunter and his Lab calling for geese, waiting for geese. (Photograph © Ron Spomer)

Real Hunting Comfort

**HUNTING COAT
AND BREECHES**

RIDING BREECHES

HUNTING VEST

Duxbak Hunting Togs are standbys with all hunters, especially old timers, because they have found *Duxbak* has been designed for comfort by sportsmen. *Duxbak* is warm, exceptionally tough, has every convenience hunters appreciate, and is rainproofed. *Kamp-it*, not rainproofed, and a little lighter in weight, is usually preferred by ladies.

Our free 1922 style book shows the many garments designed for every outdoor pastime: it's free. Get a copy from your dealer. If he can't supply you, write us.

UTICA-DUXBAK CORP.   5 Hickory Street, Utica N. Y.

**MIDDY BLOUSE
AND BREECHES**

NORFOLK AND SHELL SKIRT

EXCERPT FROM "TONTO BASIN"

By Zane Grey

One of the most popular novelists in American history, Zane Grey wrote dozens of books. His first, *Betty Zane* (1903), was about his Ohio ancestors, but after the publication of *The Last of the Plainsmen* (1908), a nonfiction account of Grey's trip west with "Buffalo" Jones, the author found his niche. Numerous novels about the American West were to follow, including *Riders of the Purple Sage* (1912) and *The U.P. Trail* (1918). Many more of his tales were published after his death in 1939.

    This excerpt from "Tonto Basin," a nonfiction account of a hunt for deer, is taken from Grey's 1922 book *Tales of Lonely Trails*.

THE HOUNDS ENJOYED a well-earned rest the next day. R. C. and I, behind Haught's back, fed them all they could eat. The old hunter had a fixed idea that dogs should be kept lean and hungry so they would run bears the better. Perhaps he was right. Only I could not withstand Old Dan and Old Tom as they limped to me, begging and whining. Yet not even sore feet and hunger could rob these grand old hounds of their dignity. For an hour that morning I sat beside them in a sunny spot.

In the afternoon Copple took me on a last deer hunt for that trip. We rode down the canyon a mile, and climbed out on the west slope. Haught had described this country as a "wolf" to travel. He used that word to designate anything particularly tough. We found the ridge, covered with a dense forest, in places a matted jungle of pine saplings. These thickets were impenetrable. Heavy snows had bent the pines so that they grew at an angle. We found it necessary to skirt these thickets, and at that, sometimes had to cut our way through with our little axes. Hunting was scarcely possible under such conditions. Still we did not see any deer tracks.

Eventually we crossed this ridge, or at least the jungle part of it, and got lower down into hollows and swales full of aspens. Copple recognized country he had hunted before. We made our way up a long shallow hollow that ended in an open where lay the remains of an old log cabin, and corrals. From under a bluff bubbled a clear beautiful spring. Copple looked all around slowly, with strange expression, and at last, dismounting he knelt to drink of the spring.

"Ah-h-good!" he exclaimed, after a deep draught. "Get down an' drink. Snow water an' it never goes dry."

Indeed it was so cold it made my teeth ache, and so pure and sweet that I drank until I could hold no more. Deer and cat and bear tracks showed along the margin of clean sand. Lower down were fresh turkey tracks. A lonely spring in the woods visited by wild game! This place was singularly picturesque and beautiful. The purest drinking water is found in wild forest or on mountains. Men, cities, civilization contaminate waters that are not isolated.

Copple told me a man named Mitchell had lived in that lonely place thirty years ago. Copple, as a boy, had worked for him—had ridden wild bronchos and roped wild steers in that open, many and many a day. Something of unconscious pathos showed in Copple's eyes as he gazed around, and in his voice. We all hear the echoing footsteps of the past years! In those days Copple said the ranch was overrun by wild game, and wild horses too.

We rode on westward, to come out at length on the rim of a magnificent canyon. It was the widest and deepest and wildest gorge I had come across in this country. So deep that only a faint roar of running water reached our ears! The slopes were too steep for man, let alone a horse; and the huge cliffs and giant spruces gave it a singularly rugged appearance. We saw deer on the opposite slope. Copple led along the edge, searching for traces of an old trail where Mitchell used to drive cattle across. We did not find a trail, but we found a place where Copple said one used to be. I could see no signs of it. Here leading his horse with one hand and wielding his little axe with the other Copple started down. For my part I found going down remarkably easy. The only trouble I had was to hold on, so I would not go down like a flash. Stockings, my horse, had in a few weeks become a splendid traveler in the forest. He had learned to restrain his spirit and use his intelligence. Where-ever I led he would go and that without any fear. There is something fine in constant association with an intelligent horse under such circumstances. In bad places Stockings braced his forefeet, sat on his haunches, and slid, sometimes making me jump to get out of his way. We found the canyon bed a narrow notch, darkly rich and green, full of the melody of wild birds and murmuring brook, with huge rocks all stained gold and russet, and grass as high as our knees. Frost still lingered in the dark, cool, shady retreat; and where the sun struck a narrow strip of the gorge there was warm, sweet, dry breath of the forest. But for the most part, down here all was damp, dank, cool shadow where sunshine never reached, and where the smells were of dead leaves and wet moss and ferns and black rich earth.

Impossible we found it to ascend the other slope where we had seen the deer, so we had to ride up the canyon, a matter greatly to my liking. Copple thought I was hunting with him, but really, except to follow him, I did not think of the meaning of his slow wary advance. Only a few more days had I to roam the pine-scented forest. That ride up this deep gorge was rich in sensation. Sun and sky and breeze and forest

Muley buck and doe on the skyline. (Photograph © Len Rue, Jr.)

encompassed me. The wilderness was all about me; and I regretted when the canyon lost its splendid ruggedness, and became like the others I had traversed, and at last grew to be a shallow grassy ravine, with patches of gray aspens along the tiny brook.

As we climbed out once more, this time into an open, beautiful pine forest, with little patches of green thicket, I seemed to have been drugged by the fragrance and the color and the beauty of the wild. For when Copple called low and sharp: "Hist!" I stared uncomprehendingly at him.

"Deer!" he whispered, pointing. "Get off an' smoke 'em up!"

Something shot through me—a different kind of thrill. Ahead in the open I saw gray, graceful, wild forms trotting away. Like a flash I slid off my horse and jerked out my rifle. I ran forward a few steps. The deer had halted—were gazing at us with heads up and ears high. What a wild beautiful picture! As I raised my rifle they

seemed to move and vanish in the green. The hunter in me, roused at last, anathematized my miserable luck. I ran ahead another few steps, to be halted by Copple. "Buck!" he called, sharply. "Hurry!" Then, farther on in the open, out in the sunlight, I saw a noble stag, moving, trotting toward us. Keen, hard, fierce in my intensity, I aligned the sights upon his breast and fired. Straight forward and high he bounded, to fall with a heavy thud.

Copple's horse, startled by my shot, began to snort and plunge. "Good shot," yelled Copple. "He's our meat."

What possessed me I knew not, but I ran ahead of Copple. My eyes searched avidly the bush-dotted ground for my quarry. The rifle felt hot in my tight grip. All inside me was a tumult—eager, keen, wild excitement. The great pines, the green aisles leading away into the woods, the shadows under the thickets, the pine-pitch tang of the air, the loneliness of that

lonely forest—all these seemed familiar, sweet, beautiful, things mine alone, things seen and smelled and felt before, things . . . Then suddenly I ran right upon my deer, lying motionless, dead I thought. He appeared fairly large, with three-point antlers. I heard Copple's horse thudding the soft earth behind me, and I yelled: "I got him, Ben." That was a moment of exultation.

It ended suddenly. Something halted me. My buck, now scarcely fifteen feet from me, began to shake and struggle. He raised his head, uttering a choking gasp. I heard the flutter of blood in his throat. He raised himself on his front feet and lifted his head high, higher, until his nose pointed skyward and his antlers lay back upon his shoulders. Then a strong convulsion shook him. I heard the shuddering wrestle of his whole body. I heard the gurgle and flow of blood. Saw the smoke of fresh blood and smelled it! I saw a small red spot in his gray breast where my bullet had struck. I saw a great bloody gaping hole on his rump where the .30 Gov't expanding bullet had come out. From end to end that bullet had torn! Yet he was not dead. Straining to rise again!

I saw, felt all this in one flashing instant. And as swiftly my spirit changed. What I might have done I never knew, but most likely I would have shot him through the brain. Only a sudden action of the stag paralyzed all my force. He lowered his head. He saw me. And dying, with lungs and heart and bowels shot to shreds, he edged his stiff front feet toward me, he dragged his afterquarters, he slid, he flopped, he skittered convulsively at me. No fear in the black, distended, wild eyes!

Only hate, only terrible, wild, unquenchable spirit to live long enough to kill me! I saw it. He meant to kill me. How magnificent, how horrible this wild courage! My eyes seemed riveted upon him, as he came closer, closer. He gasped. Blood sputtered from his throat. But more terrible than agony, than imminent death was the spirit of this wild beast to slay its enemy. Inch by inch he skidded closer to me, with a convulsive quivering awful to see. No veil of the past, no scale of civilization between beast and man then! Enemies as old as the earth! I had shot him to eat, and he would kill me before he died. For me the moment was mon-

strous. No hunter was I then, but a man stricken by the spirit and mystery of life, by the agony and terror of death, by the awful strange sense that this stag would kill me.

But Copple galloped up, and drawing his revolver, he shot the deer through the head. It fell in a heap.

"Don't ever go close to a crippled deer," admonished my comrade, as he leaped off his horse. "I saw a fellow once that was near killed by a buck he'd taken for dead. . . . . Strange the way this buck half stood up. Reckon he meant bad, but he was all in. You hit him plumb center."

"Yes, Ben, it was—strange," I replied, soberly. I caught Copple's keen dark glance studying me. "When you open him up—see what my bullet did, will you?"

"All right. Help me hang him to a snag here," returned Copple, as he untied his lasso.

When we got the deer strung up I went off into the woods, and sat on a log, and contended with a queer sort of sickness until it passed away. But it left a state of mind that I knew would require me to probe into myself, and try to understand once and for all time this bloodthirsty tendency of man to kill. It would force me to try to analyze the psychology of hunting. Upon my return to Copple I found he had the buck ready to load upon his horse. His hands were bright red. He was wiping his hunting-knife on a bunch of green pine needles.

"That 150-grain soft-nose bullet is some executioner," he declared, forcefully. "Your bullet mushroomed just after it went into his breast. It tore his lung to pieces, cut open his heart, made a mess of kidneys an' paunch, an' broke his spine. An' look at this hole where it came out!"

I helped Copple heave the load on his saddle and tie it securely, and I got my hands red at the job, but I did not really look at the buck again. And upon our way back to camp I rode in the lead all the way. We reached camp before sunset, where I had to endure the felicitations of R. C. and my comrades, all of whom were delighted that at last I had gotten a buck. Takahashi smiled all over his broad brown face. "My goodnish! I awful glad! Nice fat deer!"

That night I lay awake a long time, and though

A deer-hunting party, including Idaho Governor H. C. Baldridge, winds along a mountain stream, circa 1927. (Photograph courtesy the Idaho State Historical Society, #P1995.25.27)

aware of the moan of the wind in the pines and the tinkle of the brook, and the melancholy hoot of an owl, and later the still, sad, black silence of the midnight hours, I really had no pleasure in them. My mind was active.

Boys are inherently cruel. The games they play, at least those they invent, instinctively partake of some element of brute nature. They chase, they capture, they imprison, they torture, and they kill. No secret rendezvous of a boy's pirate gang ever failed to be soaked with imaginary blood! And what group of boys have not played at being pirates? The Indian games are worse—scalping, with red-hot cinders thrown upon the bleeding head, and the terrible running of the gauntlet, and burning at the stake.

What youngster has not made wooden knives to spill the blood of his pretended enemies? Little girls play with dolls, and with toy houses, and all the implements of making a home; but sweet and dear as the little angels are they love a boy's game, and if they can through some lucky accident participate in one it is to scream and shudder and fight, indeed like the females of the species. No break here between these little mothers of doll-babies and the bloody mothers of the French Revolution, or of dusky, naked, barbarian children of a primitive day!

Boys love the chase. And that chase depends upon environment. For want of wild game they will harry a poor miserable tom-cat with sticks and stones. I belonged once to a gang of young ruffians who chased the neighbor's chickens, killed them with clubs, and cooked them in tin cans, over a hidden fire. Boys love nothing so much as to chase a squirrel or a frightened little chipmunk back and forth along a rail fence. They brandish their sticks, run and yell, dart to and fro, like young Indians. They rob bird's nests, steal the eggs, pierce them and blow them. They capture the young birds, and are not above killing the parents that fly frantically to the rescue. I knew of boys who ground captured birds to death on a grindstone. Who has not seen a boy fling stones at a helpless hop-toad?

As boys grow older to the age of reading they select, or at least love best, those stories of bloodshed and violence. Stevenson wrote that boys read for some

A hunter glasses the rolling western hills for deer. (Photograph © Ron Spomer)

element of the brute instinct in them. His two wonderful books *Treasure Island* and *Kidnapped* are full of fight and the killing of men. *Robinson Crusoe* is the only great boy's book I ever read that did not owe its charm to fighting. But still did not old Crusoe fight to live on his lonely island? And this wonderful tale is full of hunting, and has at the end the battle with cannibals.

When lads grow up they become hunters, almost without exception, at least in spirit if not in deed. Early days and environment decide whether or not a man becomes a hunter. In all my life I have met only two grown men who did not care to go prowling and hunting in the woods with a gun. An exception proves a great deal, but all the same most men, whether they have a chance or not, love to hunt. Hunters, therefore, there are of many degrees. Hunters of the lowly cotton-tail and the woodland squirrel; hunters of quail, woodcock, and grouse; hunters of wild ducks and geese; hunters of foxes—the red-coated English and the home-spun clad American; hunters—which is a kinder name for trappers—of beaver, marten, otter, mink, all the furred animals; hunters of deer, cat, wolf, bear, antelope, elk, moose, caribou; hunters of the barren lands where the ice is king and where there are polar bears, white foxes, musk-ox, walrus. Hunters of different animals of different countries. African hunters for lion, rhinoceros, elephant, buffalo, eland, hartebeest, giraffe, and a hundred species made known to all the world by such classical sportsmen as Selous, Roosevelt, Stewart Edward White.

But they are all hunters and their game is the deadly chase in the open or the wild. There are hunters who hate action, who hate to walk and climb and toil and wear themselves out to get a shot. Such men are hunters still, but still not men! There are hunters who have game driven up to them. I heard a story told by an officer whom I believe. In the early days of the war he found himself somewhere on the border between Austria and Germany. He was invited to a hunt by

BELOW: *The end of a long day afield in pursuit of big game. (Photograph © Alan and Sandy Carey)*

FACING PAGE: *A muley in an autumn field. (Photograph © Rich Kirchner/The Green Agency)*

ABOVE: *Buck Hoist ad, 1939.*

RIGHT: *Winchester .30-.30 rifle, Winchester Super X cartridges, and other hunting equipment. (Photograph © Mark Kayser)*

personages of high degree. They motored to a sequestered palace in the forest, and next day motored to a shooting-lodge. At daylight he was called, and taken to the edge of a forest and stationed in an open glade. His stand was an upholstered divan placed high in the forks of a tree. His guide told him that pretty soon a doe would come out of the forest. But he was not to shoot it. In fifteen minutes a lame buck would come out. But he was not to shoot that one either. In ten more minutes another buck would come out, and this third deer he was to kill. My informant told me this was all very seriously meant. The gun given him was large enough in calibre to kill an elephant. He walked up the steps to the comfortable divan and settled himself to await events.

The doe trotted out exactly on schedule time. So did the lame buck. They came from the woods and were not frightened. The third deer, a large buck, was a few moments late—three minutes to be exact. According to instructions the American killed this buck—a matter that took some nerve he said, for the buck walked out like a cow. That night a big supper was given in the guest's honor. He had to eat certain parts of the buck he had killed, and drink flagons of wine. This kind of hunting must be peculiarly German or Austrian, and illustrates the peculiar hunting ways of men.

A celebrated bear hunter and guide of the northwest told me that for twenty years he had been taking eastern ministers—preachers of the gospel—on hunting trips into the wild. He assured me that of all the bloody murderers—waders in gore, as he expressed it— these teachers of the gospel were the worst. The moment they got out into the wild they wanted to kill, kill, kill. He averred their natures seemed utterly to change.

In reading the books of hunters and in listening to their talks at Camp-fire Club dinners I have always been struck with the expression of what these hunters felt, what they thought they got out of hunting. The change from city to the open wilderness; the difference between noise, tumult, dirt, foul air, and the silence, the quiet, the cleanness and purity; the sweet breath of God's country as so many called it; the beauty of forest and mountain; the wildness of ridge and valley; the wonder of wild animals in their native haunts; and the zest, the joy, the excitement, the magnificent thrill of the stalk and the chase. No one of them ever dwelt upon the kill! It was mentioned, as a result, an end, a consummation. How strange that hunters believed these were the attractions of the chase! They felt them, to be sure, in some degree, or they would not remember them. But they never realized that these sensations were only incidental to hunting.

Men take long rides, hundreds and thousands of miles, to hunt. They endure hardships, live in camps with absolute joy. They stalk through the forest, climb the craggy peaks, labor as giants in the building of the pyramids, all with a tight clutch on a deadly rifle. They are keen, intent, strained, quiveringly eager all with a tight clutch on a deadly rifle. If hunters think while on a stalk—which matter I doubt considerably—they think about the lay of the land, or the aspect of it, of the habits and possibilities of their quarry, of their labor and chances, and particularly of the vague unrealized sense of comfort, pleasure, satisfaction in the moment. Tight muscles, alert eyes, stealthy steps, stalk and run and crawl and climb, breathlessness, a hot close-pressed chest, thrill on thrill, and sheer bursting riot of nerve and vein—these are the ordinary sensations and actions of a hunter. No ascent too lofty—no descent too perilous for him then, if he is a man as well as a hunter!

Take the Brazilian hunter of the jungle. He is solitary. He is sufficient to himself. He is a survival of the fittest. The number of his tribe are few. Nature sees to that. But he must eat, and therefore he hunts. He spears fish and he kills birds and beasts with a blow-gun. He

hunts to live. But the manner of his action, though more skilful, is the same as any hunter's. Likewise his sensations, perhaps more vivid because hunting for him is a matter of life or death. Take the Gaucho of Patagonia—the silent lonely Indian hunter of the Pampas. He hunts with a *bola*, a thin thong or string at each end of which is a heavy leather-covered ball of stone or iron. This the Gaucho hurls through the air at the neck or legs of his quarry. The balls fly round—the thong binds tight—it is a deadly weapon. The user of it rides and stalks and sees and throws and feels the same as any other hunter. Time and place, weapon and game have little to do with any differences in hunters.

Up to this 1919 hunting trip in the wilds I had always marveled at the fact that naturalists and biologists hate sportsmen. Not hunters like the Yellow Knife Indians, or the snake-eating Bushmen of Australia, or the Terra-del-Fuegians, or even the native country rabbit-hunters—but the so-called sportsmen. Naturalists and biologists have simply learned the truth why men hunt, and that when it is done in the name of sport, or for sensation, it is a degenerate business. Stevenson wrote beautiful words about "the hunter home from the hill," but so far as I can find out he never killed anything himself. He was concerned with the romance of the thought, with alliteration, and the singular charm of the truth—sunset and the end of the day, the hunter's plod down the hill to the cottage, to the home where wife and children awaited him. Indeed it is a beautiful truth, and not altogether in the past, for there are still farmers and pioneers.

Hunting is a savage primordial instinct inherited from our ancestors. It goes back through all the ages of man, and farther still—to the age when man was not man, but hairy ape, or some other beast from which we are descended. To kill is in the very marrow of our bones. If man after he developed into human state had taken to vegetable diet—which he never did take—he yet would have inherited the flesh-eating instincts of his animal forebears. And no instinct is ever wholly eradicated. But man was a meat eater. By brute strength, by sagacity, by endurance he killed in order to get the means of subsistence. If he did not kill he starved. And it is a matter of record, even down to modern times, that man has existed by cannibalism.

The cave-man stalked from his hole under a cliff, boldly forth with his huge club or stone mace. Perhaps he stole his neighbor's woman, but if so he had more reason to hunt than before—he had to feed her as well as himself. This cave-man, savagely descended, savagely surrounded, must have had to hunt all the daylight hours and surely had to fight to kill his food, or to keep it after he killed it. Long, long ages was the being called caveman in developing; more long ages he lived on the earth, in that dim dark mystic past; and just as long were his descendants growing into another and higher type of barbarian. But they and their children and grandchildren, and all their successive, innumerable, and varying descendants had to hunt meat and eat meat to live.

The brain of barbarian man was small, as shown by the size and shape of his skull, but there is no reason to believe its construction and use were any different from the use of other organs—the eye to see with—the ear to hear with—the palate to taste with. Whatever the brain of primitive man was it held at birth unlimited and innumerable instincts like those of its progenitors; and round and smooth in babyhood, as it was, it surely gathered its sensations, one after another in separate and habitual channels, until when manhood arrived it had its convolutions, its folds and wrinkles. And if instinct and tendency were born in the brain how truly must they be a part of bone, tissue, blood.

We cannot escape our inheritance. Civilization is merely a veneer, a thin-skinned polish over the savage and crude nature. Fear, anger, lust, the three great primal instincts are restrained, but they live powerfully in the breast of man. Self preservation is the first law of human life, and is included in fear. Fear of death is the first instinct. Then if for thousands, perhaps millions of years, man had to hunt because of his fear of death, had to kill meat to survive—consider the ineradicable and permanent nature of the instinct.

The secret now of the instinctive joy and thrill and wildness of the chase lies clear.

Stealing through the forest or along the mountain slope, eyes roving, ears sensitive to all vibrations of the air, nose as keen as that of a hound, hands tight on a deadly rifle, we unconsciously go back. We go back to the primitive, to the savage state of man. Therein lies the joy. How sweet, vague, unreal those sensations of strange familiarity with wild places we know we never saw before! But a million years before that hour a hairy ancestor of ours felt the same way in the same kind of a place, and in us that instinct survives. That is the secret of the wonderful strange charm of wild places, of the barren rocks of the desert wilderness, of the great-walled lonely canyons. Something now in our blood, in our bones once danced in men who lived then in similar places. And lived by hunting!

The child is father to the man. In the light of this instinct how easy to understand his boyish cruelty. He is true to nature. Unlimited and infinite in his imagination when he hunts—whether with his toys or with real weapons. If he flings a stone and kills a toad he is instinctively killing meat for his home in the cave. How little difference between the lad and the man! For a man the most poignantly exciting, the most thrillingly wild is the chase when he is weaponless, when he runs and kills his quarry with a club. Here we have the essence of the matter. The hunter is proudest of his achievement in which he has not had the help of deadly weapons. Unconsciously he will brag and glow over that conquest wherein lay greatest peril to him—when he had nothing but his naked hands. What a hot gush of blood bursts over him! He goes back to his barbarian state when a man only felt. The savage lived in his sensations. He saw, heard, smelled, tasted, touched, but seldom thought. The earthy, the elemental of eye and ear and skin surrounded him. When the man goes into the wilderness to change into a hunter that surviving kinship with the savage revives in his being, and all unconsciously dominates him with driving passion. Passion it is because for long he has been restrained in the public haunts of men. His real nature has been hidden. The hunting of game inhibits his thoughts. He feels only. He forgets himself. He sees the track, he hears the stealthy step, he smells the wild scent; and his blood dances with the dance of the ages. Then he is a killer. Then the ages roll back. Then he is brother to the savage. Then all unconsciously he lives the chase, the fight, the death—dealing moment as they were lived by all his ancestors down through the misty past.

What then should be the attitude of a thoughtful man toward this liberation of an instinct—that is to say, toward the game or sport or habit of hunting to kill?

Hunters at Cardinal Falls near Mountain Park, Alberta, Canada, 1922. (Photograph courtesy the Provincial Archives of Alberta, #CL.178)

Not easily could I decide this for myself. After all life is a battle. Eternally we are compelled to fight. If we do not fight, if we do not keep our bodies strong, supple, healthy, soon we succumb to some germ or other that gets a hold in our blood or lungs and fights for its life, its species, until it kills us. Fight therefore is absolutely necessary to long life, and Alas! eventually that fight must be lost. The savages, the Babylonians, the Persians, the Greeks all worshipped physical prowess in man. Manhood, strength—the symbols of fight! To be physically strong and well a man must work hard, with frequent intervals of change of exercise, and he must eat meat. I am not a great meat eater, but I doubt if I could do much physical labor or any brain work on a vegetable diet. Therefore I hold it fair and manly to go once a year to the wilderness to hunt. Let that hunt be clean hard toil, as hard as I can stand! Perhaps nature created the lower animals for the use of man. If I had been the creator I think I would have made it possible for the so-called higher animal man to live on air.

Somewhere I read a strange remarkable story about monkeys and priests in the jungle of India. An old order of priests had from time out of mind sent two of their comrades into the jungle to live with the monkeys, to tame them, feed them, study them, love them. And these priests told an incredible story, yet one that haunted with its possibilities of truth. After a long term of years in which one certain priest had lived with the monkeys and they had learned truly he meant them no harm and only loved them, at rare moments an old monkey would come to him and weep and weep in the most terrible and tragic manner. This monkey wanted to tell something, but could not speak. But the priest knew that the monkey was trying to tell him how once the monkey people had been human like him. Only they had retrograded in the strange scale of evolution. And the terrible weeping was for loss—loss of physical stature, of speech, perhaps of soul.

What a profound and stunning idea! Does evolution work backward? Could nature in its relentless inscrutable design for the unattainable perfection have developed man only to start him backward toward the dim ages whence he sprang? Who knows! But every man can love wild animals. Every man can study and try to understand the intelligence of his horse, the loyalty of his dog. And every hunter can hunt less with his instinct, and more with an understanding of his needs, and a consideration for the beasts only the creator knows.

Driftwood campfire. (Photograph © Ron Spomer)

Hunterwear

Finding outing togs that would keep a hunter warm, dry, comfortable, or even afloat has always been a concern for serious outdoors-people. Since the rise of the sporting magazines in the late-1800s, clothing manufacturers have tried to convince hunters that their clothing line will do all of this—and more.

REMEMBERING SHOOTING-FLYING: A KEY WEST LETTER

By Ernest Hemingway

Winner of both the Pulitzer Prize and the Nobel Prize, and author of *The Sun Also Rises* (1926), *A Farewell To Arms* (1929), *For Whom the Bell Tolls* (1940), and *The Old Man and the Sea* (1952), Ernest Hemingway is an American literary figure with few, if any, peers. He was also an avid sportsman, having learned the arts of wing-shooting and fly-fishing from his father, and having honed his skills as a boy during trips to the family cabin in Michigan. He would go on to establish quite a reputation as a hunter and fisherman during the height of his literary career, and to pen the *Green Hills of Africa* (1935) and the short stories "The Snows of Kilimanjaro" (1936) and "The Short Happy Life of Francis Macomber" (1936), which were all based on Hemingway's big-game safari to Africa during the winter of 1933–1934.

"Remembering Shooting-Flying: A Key West Letter" first appeared in *Esquire* magazine in February 1935, part of a series of articles Hemingway wrote for the magazine in the 1930s.

A 1932 Ithaca 10-gauge magnum waterfowling shotgun. (Photograph © William W. Headrick)

THERE IS A heavy norther blowing; the gulf is too rough to fish and there is no shooting now. When you are through work it is nearly dark and you can ride out on the boulevard by the sea and throw clay targets with a hand trap against this gale and they will dip and jump and rise into strange angles like a jacksnipe in the wind. Or you can throw them out with the gale behind them and they will go like a teal over the water. Or you can get down below the sea wall and have some one throw them out high over your head riding the wind, but if you puff one into black dust you can not pretend it was an old cock pheasant unless you are a better pretender than I am. The trouble is there isn't any thud, nor is there the line of bare trees, nor are you standing on a wet, leaf-strewn road, nor do you hear the beaters, nor the racket when a cock gets up and, as he tops the trees, you are on him, then ahead of him, and at the shot he turns over and there is that thump when he lands. Shooting driven pheasants is worth whatever you pay for it.

But when you cannot shoot you can remember shooting and I would rather stay home, now, this afternoon and write about it than go out and sail clay saucers in the wind, trying to break them and wishing they were what they're not.

When you have been lucky in your life you find that just about the time the best of the books run out (and I would rather read again for the first time *Anna Karenina*, *Far Away and Long Ago*, *Buddenbrooks*, *Wuthering Heights*, *Madame Bovary*, *War and Peace*, *A Sportsman's Sketches*, *The Brothers Karamazov*, *Hail and Farewell*, *Huckleberry Finn*, *Winesburg, Ohio*, *La Reine Margot*, *La Maison Tellier*, *Le Rouge et le Noire*, *La Chartreuse de Parme*, *Dubliners*, Yeats's *Autobiographies* and a few others than have an assured income of a million dollars a year) you have a lot of damned fine things that you can remember. Then when the time is over in which you have done the things that you can now remember, and while you are doing other things, you find that you can read the books again and, always, there are a few, a very few, good new ones. Last year there was *La Condition Humaine* by André Malraux. It was translated, I do not know how well, as *Man's Fate,* and sometimes it is as good as Stendhal and that is something no prose writer has been in France for over fifty years.

But this is supposed to be about shooting, not about books, although some of the best shooting I remember was in Tolstoi and I have often wondered how the snipe fly in Russia now and whether shooting pheasants is counter-revolutionary. When you have loved three things all your life, from the earliest you can remember; to fish, to shoot and, later, to read; and when, all your life, the necessity to write has been your master, you learn to remember and, when you think back you remember more fishing and shooting and reading than anything else and that is a pleasure.

You can remember the first snipe you ever hit walking on the prairie with your father. How the jacksnipe rose with a jump and you hit him on the second swerve and had to wade out into a slough after him and brought him in wet, holding him by the bill, as proud as a bird dog, and you can remember all the snipe since in many places. You can remember the miracle it seemed when you hit your first pheasant when he roared up from under your feet to top a sweet briar thicket and fell with his wings pounding and you had to wait till after dark to bring him into town because they were protected, and you can feel the bulk of him still inside your shirt with his long tail up under your armpit, walking in to town in the dark along the dirt road that is now North Avenue where the gypsy wagons used to camp when there was prairie out to the Des Plaines river where Wallace Evans had a game farm and the big woods ran along the river where the Indian mounds were.

I came by there five years ago and where I shot that pheasant there was a hot dog place and filling station and the north prairie, where we hunted snipe in the spring and skated on the sloughs when they froze in the winter, was all a subdivision of mean houses, and in the town, the house where I was born was gone and they had cut down the oak trees and built an apartment house close out against the street. So I was glad I went away from there as soon as I did. Because when you like to shoot and fish you have to move often and always further out and it doesn't make any difference what they do when you are gone.

The first covey of partridges I ever saw, they were ruffed grouse but we called them partridges up there, was with my father and an Indian named Simon Green and we came on them dusting and feeding in the sun beside the grist mill on Horton's Creek in Michigan. They looked as big as turkeys to me and I was so excited with the whirr of the wings that I missed both

Pheasant *(1998) by Bob White. (Courtesy of the artist)*

shots I had, while my father, shooting an old lever ac-tion Winchester pump, killed five out of the covey and I can remember the Indian picking them up and laugh-ing. He was an old fat Indian, a great admirer of my father, and when I look back at that shooting I am a great admirer of my father too. He was a beautiful shot, one of the fastest I have ever seen; but he was too ner-vous to be a great money shot.

Then I remember shooting quail with him when I do not think I could have been more than ten years old, and he was showing me off, having me shoot pi-geons that were flying around a barn, and some way I broke the hammer spring in my single barrel 20 gauge and the only gun down there at my Uncle's place in Southern Illinois that no one was shooting, was a big old L. C. Smith double that weighed, probably, about nine pounds. I could not hit anything with it and it kicked me so it made my nose bleed. I was afraid to shoot it and I got awfully tired carrying it and my fa-ther had left me standing in a thickety patch of timber while he was working out the singles from a covey we had scattered. There was a red bird up in a tree and then I looked down and under the tree was a quail, freshly dead. I picked it up and it was still warm. My

father had evidently hit it when the covey went up with a stray pellet and it had flown this far and dropped. I looked around to see nobody was in sight and then, laying the quail down by my feet, shut both my eyes and pulled the trigger on that old double barrel. It kicked me against the tree and when I opened it up I found it had doubled and fired both barrels at once and my ears were ringing and my nose was bleeding. But I picked the quail up, reloaded the gun, wiped my nose and set out to find my father. I was sick of not hitting any.

"Did you get one, Ernie?"

I held it up.

"It's a cock," he said. "See his white throat? It's a beauty."

But I had a lump in my stomach that felt like a baseball from lying to him and that night I remember crying with my head under the patchwork quilt after he was asleep because I had lied to him. If he would have waked up I would have told him, I think. But he was tired and sleeping heavily. I never told him.

So I won't think any more about that but I re-member now how I broke the spring in the 20 gauge. It was from snapping the hammer on an empty chamber practicing swinging on the pigeons after they wouldn't let me shoot any more. And some older boys came along the road when I was carrying the pigeons from the barn to the house and one of them said I didn't shoot those pigeons. I called him a liar and the smaller of the two whipped hell out of me. That was an unlucky trip.

On a day as cold as this you can remember duck shooting in the blind, hearing their wings go whichy-chu-chu-chu in the dark before daylight. That is the first thing I remember of ducks; the whistly, silk tearing sound the fast wingbeats make; just as what you remember first of geese is how slow they seem to go when they are traveling, and yet they are moving so fast that the first one you ever killed was two behind the one you shot at, and all that night you kept waking up and remembering how he folded up and fell. While the woodcock is an easy bird to hit, with a soft flight like an owl, and if you do miss him he will probably pitch down and give you another shot. But what a bird to eat flambé with armagnac cooked in his own juice and butter, a little mustard added to make a sauce, with two strips of bacon and pommes soufflé and Corton, Pommard, Beaune, or Chambertin to drink.

Now it is colder still and we found ptarmigan in the rocks on a high plain above and to the left of the glacier by the Madelener-haus in the Vorarlberg with it blowing a blizzard and the next day we followed a fox track all day on skis and saw where he had caught a ptarmigan underneath the snow. We never saw the fox.

There were chamois up in that country too and black cock in the woods below the timber-line and big hares that you found sometimes at night when we were coming home along the road. We ate them jugged and drank Tyroler wine. And why, today, remember misses?

There were lots of partridges outside of Constantinople and we used to have them roasted and start the meal with a bowl of caviar, the kind you never will be able to afford again, pale grey, the grains as big as buck shot and a little vodka with it, and then the partridges, not overdone, so that when you cut them there was the juice, drinking Caucasus burgundy, and serving French fried potatoes with them and then a salad with roquefort dressing and another bottle of what was the number of that wine? They all had numbers. Sixty-one I think it was.

And did you ever see the quick, smooth lifting, reaching flight the lesser bustard has, or make a double on them, right and left, or shoot at flighting sand grouse coming to water early in the morning and see the great variety of shots they give and hear the cackling sound they make when flighting, a little like the noise of prairie chickens on the plains when they go off, fast beat of wings and soar, fast beat of wings and soar stiff-winged, and see a coyote watching you a long way out of range and see an antelope turn and stare and lift his head when he hears the shotgun thud? Sand grouse, of course, fly nothing like a prairie chicken. They have a cutting, swooping flight like pigeons but they make that grouse-like cackle, and with the lesser bustard and the teal, there is no bird to beat them for pan, the griddle or the oven.

So you recall a curlew that came in along the beach one time in a storm when you were shooting plover, and jumping teal along a water course that cut a plain on a different continent, and having a hyena come out of the grass when you were trying to stalk up on a pool and see him turn and look at ten yards and let him have it with the shotgun in his ugly face, and standing, to your waist in water,

A day afield near Banff, Alberta, Canada, 1928. (Photograph courtesy the Provincial Archives of Alberta, #A.3939)

Pintails Decoyed *(1921) by Frank W. Benson. (Courtesy Museum of Fine Arts, Boston)*

whistling a flock of golden plover back, and then, back in the winter woods, shooting ruffed grouse along a trout stream where only an otter fished now, and all the places and the different flights of birds, jumping three mallards now, down where the beavers cut away the cottonwoods, and seeing the drake tower, white-breasted, green-headed, climbing and get above him and splash him in the old Clark's Fork, walking along the bank watching him until he floated onto a pebbly bar.

Then there are sage hens, wild as hawks that time, the biggest grouse of all, getting up out of range, and out of range, until you came around an alfalfa stack and four whirred up one after the other at your feet almost and, later walking home, in your hunting coat they seemed to weigh a ton.

I think they all were made to shoot because if they were not why did they give them that whirr of wings that moves you suddenly more than any love of country? Why did they make them all so good to eat and why did they make the ones with silent flight like wood-cock, snipe, and lesser bustard, better eating even than the rest?

Why does the curlew have that voice, and who thought up the plover's call, which takes the place of noise of wings, to give us that catharsis wing shooting has given to men since they stopped flying hawks and took to fowling pieces? I think that they were made to shoot and some of us were made to shoot them and if that is not so well, never say we did not tell you that we liked it.

ABOVE: *It is quite doubtful that Hallmark would offer Christmas Cards for Men today, but in 1946, the line was touted in full-color ads in major outdoors magazines.*

RIGHT: *Duck hunter and dog prepare for the morning hunt.* *(Photograph © Bill Marchel)*

WHY I TAUGHT MY BOYS TO BE HUNTERS

By Archibald Rutledge

Archibald Rutledge was a writer with the South in his soul. His plantation home in South Carolina figures prominently in much of his outdoors writing, and his style reflects the South of his lifetime (1883–1973) in all its glory—and prejudices. A versatile writer, he penned poetry, fiction, and nonfiction; in fact, he is both the poet laureate of South Carolina and a recipient of the John Burroughs Medal for nature writing. He contributed more than a thousand articles and poems to magazines and was the author of dozens of books, including *Old Plantation Days* (1911), *Plantation Game Trails* (1921), *Bolio and Other Dogs* (1930), *Hunter's Choice* (1946), and *Those Were the Days* (1955).

"Why I Taught My Boys To Be Hunters" was first published in *An American Hunter* and also appeared in Jim Casada's anthology of Rutledge's work, *Hunting & Home in the Southern Heartland*.

A boy returns from a hunt, Knox County, Kentucky, 1940. (Photograph courtesy the Library of Congress)

I HAVE SAID that my hunting has often been solitary; but that was chiefly in the early days. During the last twenty-five years I have rarely taken to the woods and fields in the shooting season without having one or more of my own sons with me. Few human relationships are closer than those established by a mutual contact with nature; and it has always seemed to me that if more fathers were woodsmen, and would teach their sons to be likewise, most of the so-called father-and-son problems would vanish.

Providence gave me three sons, only about a year and a half apart; and since it was not possible for me to give them what we usually call the advantages of wealth, I made up my mind to do my best by them. I decided primarily to make them sportsmen, for I have a conviction that to be a sportsman is a mighty long step in the direction of being a man. I thought also that if a man brings up his sons to be hunters, they will never grow away from him. Rather the passing years will only bring them closer, with a thousand happy memories of the woods and fields. Again, a hunter never sits around home forlornly, not knowing what in the world to do with his leisure. His interest in nature will be such that he can delight in every season, and he has resources within himself that will make life always seem worth while.

Hunters should be started early. As each one of my boys reached the age of six I gave him a single-shot .22 rifle, and I began to let him go afield with me. For a year or so I never let him load the gun, even with dust shot; but I just tried to give him some notions of how to handle it, of how to cross a ditch or a fence with it, and in what direction to keep the muzzle pointed.

It was a great day for each youngster when he shot his first English sparrow with a .22 shot shell.

From the time when the first one was six years old, I could never get into my hunting clothes without hearing, "Dad, take me along!" Sometimes an argument was added: "I will shoot straight. I will put it on him!" To these winning pleas I have always tried to give an affirmative answer, even when I had to alternate carrying a played-out boy and a played-out puppy. But I knew that I was on the right track when I was trying to impress on the younger generation the importance of shooting straight. I directly applied to my own children that old copy-book maxim, "Teach the young idea how to shoot." I think the rod and gun better for boys than the saxophone and the fudge sundae. In the first place, there is something inherently manly and home-bred and truly American in that expression, "shooting straight." The hunter learns that reward comes from hard work; he learns from dealing with nature that a man must have a deep respect for the great natural laws. He learns also, I think, in a far higher degree than any form of standardized amateur athletics can give him, to play the game fairly.

Most of our harmless and genuine joys in this life are those which find their source in primitive instincts. A man who follows his natural inclinations, with due deference to common sense and moderation, is usually on the right track. Now the sport of hunting is one of the most honorable of the primeval instincts of man. What human thrill is there in lounging into a grimy butcher-shop and sorrowfully surrendering a hard-earned simoleon for a dubious slab of inert beef? Certainly any true man would far rather trudge fifteen miles in inclement weather just for a chance at a grouse. Even if he gets nothing, he will be a younger and a better man when he gets home, and with memories that will lighten the burden of the days when he cannot go afield.

A lot of good people, seeing me rearing my sons to be woodsmen, have offered me advice. "How can you love nature and yet shoot a deer?" "How can you bear to teach those children to kill things?"

These parlor naturalists and lollypop sentimentalists, whose knowledge of nature is such that they would probably take a flying buttress for a lovely game bird, are incapable of understanding that it is far less cruel to kill a wild deer than it is to poleax a defenseless ox in a stall. The ox has no chance; but the deer has about four chances out of five against even the good hunter. Besides, I have a philosophy which teaches me that certain game birds and animals are apparently made to be hunted, because of their peculiar food value and because their character lends zest to the pursuit of them. It has never seemed to me to be too far-fetched to suppose that Providence placed game here for a special purpose.

Hunting is not incompatible with the deepest and most genuine love of nature. Audubon was something of a hunter; so was the famous Bachman; so were both John Muir and John Burroughs. It has always seemed

A proud boy shows his father his bagged mourning dove. (Photograph © Bill Marchel)

to me that any man is a better man for being a hunter. This sport confers a certain constant alertness, and develops a certain ruggedness of character that, in these days of too much civilization, is refreshing; moreover, it allies us to the pioneer past. In a deep sense, this great land of ours was won for us by hunters.

Again, there is a comradeship among hunters that has always seemed to me one of the finest human relationships. When fellow sportsmen meet in the woods or fields or the lonely marshes, they meet as friends who understand each other. There is a fine democracy about all this that is a mighty wholesome thing for young people to know. As much as I do anything else

in life I treasure my comradeships with old, grizzled woodsmen. Hunting alone could have made us friends. And I want my boys to go through life making these humble contacts and learning from fellow human beings, many of them very unpretentious and simplehearted, some of the ancient lore of nature that is one of the very finest heritages of our race. Nature always solves her own problems; and we can go far toward solving our own if we will listen to her teachings and consort with those who love her.

In the case of my own boys, from the .22 rifle they graduated to the .410 shotgun; then to a 20-gauge; then a 16; then a 12. I was guide for my oldest son,

Arch, when he shot his first stag. We stalked him at sundown on Bull's Island, in the great sea-marsh of that magnificent preserve, creeping through the bulrushes and the myrtle bushes until we got in a position for a shot. And that night at the clubhouse, when I went to bed late, I found my young hunter still wide awake, no doubt going over our whole campaign of that memorable afternoon.

I was near my second son, Middleton, when he shot his first five stags. I saw all of them fall—and these deeds were done before he was eighteen.

I followed the blood-trail of the first buck my youngest son, Irvine, shot. He had let drive one barrel of his 16-gauge at this great stag in a dense pine thicket. The buck made a right-about face and headed for the river, a mile away. He was running with a doe, and she went on across the water. The buck must have known that he could not make it, for he turned up the plantation avenue, actually jumped the gate, splashing it with blood, and fell dead under a giant live-oak only eighty yards from the house!

It's one thing to kill a deer, and it's another to kill one and then have him accommodate you by running out of the wilds right up to your front steps. That kind of performance saves a lot of toting. This stag was an old swamp buck with massive antlers. Last Christmas my eldest son had only three days' vacation; but he got two bucks.

Yes, I have brought up my three boys to be hunters; and I know full well that when the wild creatures need no longer have any apprehensions about me, my grandchildren will be hard on their trail, pursuing with keen enjoyment and wholesome passion the sport of kings. While other boys are whirling in the latest jazz or telling dubious stories on street corners, I'd like to think that mine are deep in the lonely woods, far in the silent hills, listening to another kind of music, learning a different kind of lore.

This privilege of hunting is about as fine a heritage as we have, and it needs to be passed on unsullied from father to son. There is still hope for the race when

Wary whitetails on the edge of the woods. (Photograph © Bill Marchel)

some members of it are not wholly dependent upon effete and urbane artificialities for their recreation. A true hunter will never feel at home in a night club. The whole thing would seem to him rather pathetic and comical—somehow not in the same world with solitary fragrant woods, rushing rivers and the elegant high-born creatures of nature with which he is familiar. Hunting gives a man a sense of balance, a sanity, a comprehension of the true values of life that make vicious and crazily stimulated joy a repellent thing.

I well remember the morning when I took all three of my boys on a hunt for the first time. I had told them the night before that we were going for grouse and had to make an early start for Path Valley. There must have been a romantic appeal in the phrase "early start," for I could hardly get them to sleep that night. And

such a time as we had getting all the guns and shells and hunting clothes ready, and a lunch packed, and the alarm clock set! And now, nine years after that memorable day, we still delight in making early starts together.

That day, before we had been in the dewy fringes of the mountain a half hour, as we were walking abreast about fifty yards apart, we had the good fortune to flush a covey of five ruffed grouse. It was the first time that any of my boys had had a shot at this grand bird, which to my way of thinking outpoints every other game bird in the whole world, bar none. An old cock with a heavy ruff fell to Middleton's gun. A young cock tried to get back over Irvine's bead. It was a gallant gesture, but the little huntsman's aim was true, and down came the prince of the woodland.

Arch and I were a little out of range for a shot on the rise, but ere long we flushed other birds, and I had the satisfaction of seeing him roll his first *Bonasa umbellus*. We were walking through some second growth, which was fairly thick. I had just been telling him that in such cover a grouse is mighty likely to go up pretty fast and steep to clear the treetops, where, for the tiniest fraction of a split second, it will seem to pause as it checks its rise and the direction of its flight, which is to take it like a scared projectile above the forest. I had been telling Arch that the best chance under such circumstances was usually offered just as the grouse got above the sprouts and seemed to hesitate.

I had just taken up my position in line when out of a tangle of fallen grape-vines that had been draping a clump of sumac bushes a

LEFT: *Remington Kleanbore .22 cartridge ad, 1936.*

FACING PAGE: *1937 Wesley Richards 16-gauge shotgun and ruffed grouse.* (Photograph © Doug Stamm/ProPhoto)

regal grouse roared up in front of Arch. I could see the splendid bird streaking it for the sky and safety. At first I was afraid that Arch would shoot too soon, then that he would shoot too late; either one would be like not shooting at all. But just as the cock topped the trees and tilted himself downward the gun spoke, and the tilt continued, only steeper and without control. With a heavy thud the noble bird dropped within my sight on the tinted leaves of the autumnal forest floor.

Fellow-sportsmen will appreciate what I mean when I say that was a great day for me. When a father can see his boy follow and fairly kill our most wary and splendid game bird, I think the Old Man has a right to feel that his son's education is one to be proud of. I'd far rather have a son of mine able to climb a mountain and outwit the wary creatures of the wilderness than be able to dance the Brazilian busybody or be able to decide whether a lavender tie will match mauve socks. These little lisping men, these modern ruins, these lazy effeminates who could not tell you the difference between a bull and a bullet—it is not in these that the hope of America, that the hope of humanity, lies.

When Arch was thirteen, I had him up at daybreak with me one morning in the wilds of the Tuscarora mountains. From the crest of the wooded ridge on which we were standing we could see over an immense gorge on either side and beyond them, far away over

the rolling ridges, northward and southward. It was dawn of the first day, and there were many hunters in the mountains. The best chance at a turkey in that country at such a time is to take just such a stand and wait for one to fly over or perhaps to come walking warily up the slope of one of the leaf-strewn gullies. We had been standing together for about fifteen minutes and had heard some shooting to the northward of us, three ridges away, when I saw a great black shape coming toward us over the tree-tops.

"Here he comes, son!" I told my youthful huntsman. "Hold for his head when he gets almost over you."

Three minutes later my boy was down on the slope of the gorge, retrieving a 19-pound gobbler, as proud

as a lad could be, and entitled to be proud. It was all he could do to toil up the hill with his prize.

Irvine shot his first turkey on our plantation in Carolina. He was on a deer-stand when this old tom came running to him through the huckleberries. The great bird stood almost as tall as he did.

Middleton killed his first under peculiar circumstances. We walked into a flock together, at daybreak, and they scattered in all directions, but were too drowsy to fly far. He wounded a splendid bird, and it alighted in a tall yellow pine about a hundred yards from us. There was not enough cover to enable him to creep up to it, and the morning was so very still that I was afraid his first step would scare the gobbler from his lofty perch.

"I know what to do," he whispered to me as I stood at a loss to know what to advise. "Don't you hear that old woodpecker hammering on that dead pine? Every time he begin to rap I'm going to take an easy, soft step forward. Perhaps can get close enough."

"Go ahead," I told him, and stood watching this interesting stalk.

The woodpecker proved very accommodating, and every other minute hammered loudly on the sounding tree. Step by cautious step Middleton got nearer. At last he raised his gun, and at its report the gobbler reeled earthward. I thought the little piece of woodcraft very neatly executed.

If the sentimentalist were right, hunting would develop in men a cruelty of character. But I have found that it inculcates patience, demands discipline and iron nerve, and develops a serenity of spirit that makes for long life and long love of life. And it is my fixed conviction that if a parent can give his children a passionate and wholesome devotion to the outdoors, the fact that he cannot leave each of them fortune does not really matter so much. They will always enjoy life in its nobler aspects without money and without price. They will worship the Creator in his mighty works. And because they know and love the natural world, they will always feel at home in the wide, sweet habitations of the Ancient Mother.

Male wild turkeys display for passing females. (Photograph © Michael H. Francis)

PA'TRIDGE FEVER—
CAUSE AND CURE

By Gordon MacQuarrie

G ordon MacQuarrie was born and raised in far northern Wisconsin—as far north as you can get, in fact—in the shipping town of Superior, on the western corner of the lake by the same name. He spent the first thirteen years of his career working for the Superior *Evening Telegram,* rising from a reporter to managing editor. He married Helen Peck in Superior in 1927; Helen's father served as the inspiration for MacQuarrie's famous stories about the Old Duck Hunter's Association. In 1936, he left his boyhood home to take a job as outdoors editor of the Milwaukee *Journal,* a position he held until his death in 1956. MacQuarrie's articles and stories were widely published in *Outdoor Life*, *Field & Stream*, and *Sports Afield*, and his wonderful stories about the Old Duck Hunter's Association were published posthumously in three books, *Stories of the Old Duck Hunters and Other Drivel* (1967), *More Stories of the Old Duck Hunters* (1983), and *Last Stories of the Old Duck Hunters* (1994).

"Pa'tridge Fever—Cause and Cure" first appeared in the January 1941 issue of *Outdoor Life*.

A ruffed grouse—a "pa'tridge" in Gordon MacQuarrie's Wisconsin—drumming on an autumn day. (Photograph © Bill Marchel)

WITH AUTUMN, WHEN the world is brown and the season hesitates between smoky Indian summer and leaden November, there comes to proper hunting men an urge to scuff their feet among the curling sweet fern and poke a load or two at pa'tridge.

Anyway he's pa'tridge here in Wisconsin. No Badger hillbilly would waste time wrapping his tongue around "ruffed grouse." And if you said "Bonasa umbellus," your man of the pa'tridge woods, from the blue Baraboo hills 300 miles north to Lake Superior's shore, would think you were swearing at him. No, your better class of pa'tridge hunters in Wisconsin refer to our gallant fantail as just plain old pa'tridge—"an' dang it, neighbor, if you c'n ketch one toppin' the hardwood ye've earned 'im."

The will to go to a place where there are pa'tridge comes upon a man suddenly, inexplicably. It may happen in the midst of dense traffic. It may happen in the thick of a business conference. Your proper hunting man may have been quite complacent with the world and its things. And then, without a word of warning, as the cub reporter wrote when the cornice fell off the Masonic Temple, your proper hunting man becomes a mercuric creature of moods, soured on everything, especially hateful toward sweet old ladies and spaniel puppies.

Moneyed people in that frame of mind often make the mistake of winding up in one of those chromium offices where their unconscious selves are explored. Other kinds of people—pa'tridge hunters, for instance—people with a strong leaning toward sulphur and molasses and red-flannel underwear in season, know the remedy.

The remedy is walnut and steel, oiled leather, baggy canvas jacket, and the stinging smell of nitro hanging in the hazel brush.

Your proper hunting man standeth not upon the order of his going. And it makes no difference how far it is to The Place. He'll get there, and never give a hoot about the consequences. The only thing to do is to go, and let someone else worry about the storm windows, the World Series, or the state of the nation. The going is a very great part of it. It is the delicious prelude to the prime adventure of letting go with the right barrel on the first flushed bird.

I want you to know I had a nice day for it.

The country was exactly fine. Up through the fat, blacksoil counties of southern Wisconsin I drove. Up through the country of the vase-shaped elms, and the oaks like upturned bunches of grapes. Up and up—into the places north where the somber Puritan pines spotted the landscape, grew thicker and thicker and thicker, until finally the country was black with pines, and the elms and oaks were patchy interlopers.

I'd been tired for days, and that made it easier to loll back with a heavy foot and just panoram' right through Wisconsin from one end to the other. North up one long concrete carpet, west along another, then north once more onto the crooked fire lane, a highway in fact, a fire lane now only in name. The startled buck in his autumn sleekness leaping off the road. The lone, sinister cormorant on the rampike at the edge of the Chippewa flowage. The bouncing snowshoe rabbits, still brown. Up through the north of Wisconsin, in a warm, mellow world of gold and yellow and brown and red.

Toward the last of that drive I shifted often behind the wheel. A man has got to have a backbone to drive 360 miles fast; and how can you have a backbone after the auto-to-office and auto-to-home that we city folks go through day after day? You can't.

The fire lane ends, and the course is west again; west into the red, round setting sun, with a silty wake of sand and dust behind. West down the skinny, familiar road from the mail box, dodging the trees—and there is The Place.

The Place is in piny woods with a lemon-yellow log cabin in its center, a blue lake behind it for a back drop, a wisp of smoke from a cobblestone chimney, and a brown man in khaki trousers and a sagging, gray woolen vest waiting on the stoop for me.

The brown man was the president of the Old Duck Hunter's Association, Inc., a symbolic figure to all proper hunting men. Sometimes the president of an Old Duck Hunter's Association is a fellow named Joe, sometimes Jim, sometimes Louie. This one was Al, of the quizzical, challenging gleam in the eye and the much-chewed cigar and the traditional rainment of all the Als and Joes in pa'tridge time, right down to the khaki pants tucked into ten-inch boots, smooth on the bottoms from contact with pine needles.

"So you got here." He shook hands. "Where's the dog?"

Issuing hunting licenses in Madison, Wisconsin, 1934. (Photograph courtesy State Historical Society of Wisconsin, Neg. No. WH1 D487 24650)

Blazes! I'd forgotten it—him. The dog was to have been a shouldery setter with a back mask and a mantel-piece of trophies, whose owner had decided a day or two on pa'tridge was just what he needed, what with another field trial coming along.

"It's just like it always was," said Mister President. "I've got to do all the thinking for the association. Well, I'll show you pa'tridge without a dog. I'm glad you didn't bring him. It'd be too easy. Get out. Gimme that gun. Gimme that bag. Come on in. Sit down. Take off your shoes. Supper's almost ready. Shut up!"

God bless the presidents of the Old Duck Hunter's Associations, wherever they may be, and especially Al Peck.

He fiddled with things on a kitchen range that smelled of burning jack pine. He dropped one match on yellow birch bark beneath oaken logs, and the var-nished lemon-color cedar logs of the big room gave back the fireplace light. He relit his cigar, pushed back his chair from the spreading heat, and began:

"Boy, you've got an idea of what has been happening in your old stamping ground. Let's see, you've missed four pa'tridge seasons, and the last one was at the low point in the cycle. Since then your square-tailed friends have gone on a housekeeping rampage. There's pa'tridge in every hardwood clump I can find in southern Bayfield County. I'm not saying as many as in 1932—will you ever forget that?—but enough to prove to me that you are still a poorer wing-shot than me.

"Pa'tridge? It's a good thing the birds around here have had me to keep 'em stirred up. When the season opened two weeks ago they were so tame they wouldn't get out of the way of a car. But I learned 'em. Now I've got 'em trained so they get up thirty yards ahead of you and duck behind the first tree.

"Let's eat. What's that on your plate, did you say? God bless us, the boy has forgotten what roast pa'tridge tastes like!"

So it went. Until the owls began their lonely cries across the lake somewhere and the stars were bright and there was a rough woolen blanket under my chin and the waves on the lake shore went lap, lap, lap. . . .

Mister President was alive next morning at heaven knows what hour. It seemed only a moment before that I had closed my eyes. But there he was, yanking at the scarlet blanket and repeating such abysmal sounds as "Daylight in the swamps!"—the consequences of a well-spent youth in the logging camps of the North.

Smoke from the stovepipe is a sure sign of warmth awaiting the returning hunter. (Photograph © Ron Spomer)

There was then a thing called breakfast, but which deserves a better name when it is eaten before a fireplace beating back the early morning chill. The Hon. President even had pancakes. Did you ever eat sour-cream pancakes, made by a master hand?

There was a beginning to pa'tridge hunting. The president of the Old Duck Hunters makes a rite of such a privilege. Everything must be just so—the season, the day, the company. He laced his boots a bit tighter, pulled on a baggy, stained hunting jacket, fit the familiar little crooked pipe and stood on the cabin stoop, 16 gauge under his arm—a full and proper and capable pa'tridge hunter if I ever saw one.

Now, this is not a bad pa'tridge country when the cycle is up. It's a sandy, piny country, with some surprising patches of hardwood here and there. And best of all for the pa'tridge hunter, it is interlaced with dozens and scores of trails—old tote roads and rights of way of lumbering days.

Mister President sniffed the air. It was good air to sniff, bracing, fragrant with pine and sweet fern and the honest, dewy smell of a bright October morning. He relit his pipe and mapped the plan of action:

"We can get into the car and drive down the Hayward road. Or we can push back in from Andy's and skirt that pothole lake. Or we can mooch down the back road and turn right into the Cathedral."

The Cathedral is a grove of stately Norway pines growing in a natural amphitheater perhaps a mile from the cabin. I have seldom walked into this enchanting place in autumn without flushing pa'tridge. The President knew my weakness for this place, so it was by a sort of mutual, unspoken meeting of minds that we started for it.

The way into it is little known, and God forbid that I should map it. (One time I spoke out in meeting about a certain mallard hole.) Many people supposedly familiar with the lake country roundabout have never been into it. Mister President had well named it the Cathedral that first day, years ago, when he had stumbled into it after fighting through the dense brush country almost surrounding it. There is a feeling of reverence in your proper hunting man in such a place. Reverence, and if he has been there before, vigilant alertness, for

The SUV of its day, the 1940 Nash was "the answer to a sportman's prayer."

you never know when the brown one with the fantail will explode from the forest floor and go slanting off among the big boles.

Such mornings are not soon forgotten. The city was far, far away. The day was perfect. The President in the lead, we walked quietly out of the snaky, brushy trail into the open spaces beneath those big trees. We were in the pit of the amphitheater of Norway pines. To our right the big sticks climbed the hill, and in front of us they were there too. To our left was the beginning of a swamp.

The President worked off to my left and signaled me to advance through the wood parallel with him. The silent solemnity was broken by the thunder of wings. A brown bomb, thirty yards off, moving to my left, was heading for the swamp. Two shots and my double triggers were limp, and the bird had gained the dense spruce in safety.

The President spoke:

"Now you're gonna tell me you always did better on left-to-right shots. Well, if I'd had that shot I'd—"

A second buster climbed up and out, planing and twisting. With hardly a pause in his sermon, The President collected him and went on:

"—do it just like that!"

Modesty, to a president of the Old Duck Hunter's Association, is a becoming virtue only in children and setter pups.

Once through the grove, which I always leave with regret, we split, agreed to meet at noon in the cabin.

The brown woods took me in. The forest floor was moist below but dry and noisy above its mulch. Birds were flushing wild. The sun beat down. I saw a peculiar thing. A red squirrel, arguing with something, permitted me to come very close. I tried to reach out and touch him with my gun muzzle, and he scampered out of his tree and away. As he did so, a pa'tridge thundered up, not ten feet from me, and was gone in a grand, clattering parabola of flight before I could shoot.

The brown woods took me in again. The sun was climbing. There was a path, along the high bank of a water thoroughfare, where deer and fishermen and rabbits pass. From a dusting depression in the center of this path I took my first bird, a fantail that made the mistake of flying the thoroughfare. I collected.

Working along this high path I flushed several more far ahead. The path was too open. The birds were too wary. The President had "learned" them well. He had the pa'tridge in those woods ducking for cover at the first hint of danger. I could hear birds getting up as much as seventy and eighty yards away.

It was as The President had said—almost as good as 1932.

There was a pa'tridge year that will live long in the memory of northern Wisconsin upland gunners. It was in 1933 when the plague hit. Had Wisconsin known in 1932 what it knows now about pa'tridge, you may be sure 1932, instead of having a short season, would have had a good long one.

The idea of collecting the crop before disease collects it is firmly planted in Wisconsin. The old idea was to save for the sake of saving—an idea that was a prostitution of sound conservation. It was the carrying of a good thing too far. Wisconsin knows better now.

Each year there is a meeting in Madison, where more than 200 sportsmen from 71 counties recommend to the state conservation department the hunting and fishing laws for the ensuing year. It is a unique and highly successful method of working out the laws,

now being copied by other states, and proving with each passing year the soundness of the idea. At this meeting are the same sportsmen who, for four years, denied themselves and all others the right to hunt pa'tridge and prairie chicken, knowing the birds would have to be let alone to make a comeback—the same men who tote the grain bags through the winter drifts to feed the pheasants, while their argumentative

12-gauge Purdey with grouse tailfeathers. (Photograph © Bill Buckley/The Green Agency)

opponents are writing letters to newspapers condemning all hunters as lustful killers. And they know the thing to do is collect the crop.

The buggy-whip brush beckoned me on—alders, small birches, and dense undergrowth close to the ground. It was obvious now I must get close for a shot. It was hard work, a continual fight with slapping brush. Of the shots I missed, of the shots I tried off balance, of the foot-tangling affection of that brush, any proper pa'tridge hunter could write many paragraphs.

After a half hour of it your jacket is open. In an hour you wish you'd left the jacket home and brought only a cord with which to tie the game, if any, to your belt. The sweat pours down. You get shots. You get tries at phantom wraiths blistering up and out. You send No. 7's on futile brush-busting errands through the whip switches at canny down-drifters. You accept mean, cutting slashes from springy branches. Your eyes are shut half the time, expecting a blow. You are mighty lucky to make feathers fly on one out of four offerings.

When it was over, I had only two birds to show Mister President back at the cabin at noon. Of course he had his limit of four—"Been here waiting for you an hour." I sluiced and doused from the waist up in cold pump water, partook of Mister President's noon repast, and then helped him buck up wood. All of the presidents of the Old Duck Hunters are alike in the respect that they can't sit still. He had enough wood for months.

It was late afternoon when he looked at the sun, dropped his saw, and said "come on." To the Cathedral again of course.

What a place was that grove in the slanting rays of the dropping sun! The trees seemed bigger. The shadows were blacker. The orange bark was brighter. There hung over it the sultry smoke of Indian summer. Insects buzzed in the sunny patches, and high in the Norway tops summer was still alive. But where we stood, the cool October night was beginning to gather among the big trees.

The President, without a gun, went to the top of the amphitheater, and sat on a log like a judge. He could see every move I made down below him.

I proceeded slowly, and for once luck was on my side, for the first one zoomed straight away. It flew down an open aisle among the big trunks, and the right barrel just couldn't miss it. But I was a little bit deflated when I heard the voice of The President, from his spot on the hill: "Sissy! That pa'tridge committed suicide!"

Nevertheless he was my pa'tridge. One more now. One more to confute the President. I was almost through the grove when the second bird flushed, exactly like the first, straight away.

You know how those gift shots are. Nothing to it. Take it easy. Take all the time in the world. Be deliberate. Be cocksure. I think I even posed a little bit for the benefit of The President. I'd show him. I'd make him eat his words.

The crack of nitro in the Cathedral was thunderous. Once, twice I fired. Nothing happened. The pa'tridge vanished in the spruce swamp. I stood there in the pit of the grove, embarrassed to the ears, and heard the judgment from on high:

"Four feet closer and you'd have had him—maybe."

The pa'tridge day was over. We stood a minute looking down into that splendid grove. The spell of the place had hold of me. I told him that some day I wanted to stand right there where we were and let him drive a buck to me out of the spruce swamp. I told him I'd wait for the buck to emerge from the dark spruce, edge into the grove and perhaps offer me a running shot. And there I'd be—waiting.

Mister President studied the layout below. He studied the place where the last pa'tridge had vanished. Then he studied me and said:

"You might get him. Yessir, you might. But how about you doing the driving and me the shooting?"

Harrington & Richardson Arms Company ad, March 1945.

The War Years

From 1941 to 1945, the United States and its Allies battled Nazi Germany and Imperial Japan in World War II. America's industrial might swung behind the war effort, and most citizens felt it was their patriotic duty to support the troops in any way possible. Makers of guns and other hunting equipment also contributed greatly to the Allied forces, manufacturing products for the military on a never-before-seen scale. Manufacturers ran ads touting their efforts to support the Allies, including many public relations ads informing Americans that the company's entire operations had been switched over to war production.

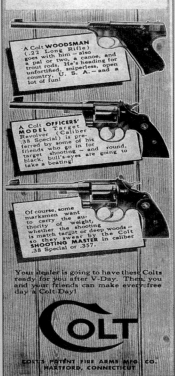

ABOVE: *Savage Arms Corporation ad, April 1943.*

LEFT: *Colt ad, May 1945, published shortly before the end of the war in Europe.*

Redfield Gunsight Corporation ad, December 1943.

SHIFT OF THE WIND

By Sigurd F. Olson

Sigurd Olson wrote poignantly of the natural world that surrounded his home in Ely, Minnesota, just a few lakes down from the Canadian border. A naturalist, Olson headed the biology department of the Ely Community College before becoming dean of the school in 1936. He later left academia to write full time, and also served as a consultant to the U.S. Department of Interior and other governmental and nongovernmental organizations working for wildlife.

Sigurd Olson was also a hunter. Stories of his pursuits appeared in *Sports Afield*, *Outdoor Life*, *Field & Stream*, and other magazines, and also were included in many of his books, including *The Singing Wilderness* (1956), *Listening Point* (1958), and others.

"Shift of the Wind" was first published in the December 1944 issue of *Sports Afield*.

Calling for ducks, 1944. (Photograph courtesy the North Carolina Division of Archives and History)

MY MIND WAS made up. I would work all day Saturday and might even go to church Sunday morning. The more I thought about it, the more indecisive and masterful I became. My old gypsy ways were over. I was to see that there was infinitely more satisfaction in getting a host of long-neglected jobs out of the way than in heading for the rice beds to what I knew would be just another fiasco as far as ducks were concerned. I felt virtuous and substantial. This weekend I'd stay home.

But as the days passed and Friday night was only a matter of hours away, a strange excitement filled my being. I had a feeling that something unusual was going to happen and I was never one to take my hunches lightly. There was, I began to sense, just the barest ghost of a chance that the wind might shift for perhaps an hour, just long enough to make them uneasy. One shot would be enough, one last flock careening over the decoys.

Another thing, it was getting late. October was getting well along and though the weather wasn't ripe, it was the time of year when anything might happen and wouldn't it be criminal to be caught with a shovel in one's hand or pushing a wheelbarrow with the flight coming down? And this I knew, too, that when the ducks did come, they would come with a rush. All they needed was a jittery temperature and a shift of the breeze to send them hurtling down out of the north.

And though the days for a month had been warm, I knew the snow soon would be flying and then it would be all over, portages covered with yellowing leaves, the rice beds blue and gold. There was just a chance something might happen and it wouldn't hurt to take a little swing around to look things over. If there was nothing doing, I would turn right around and come back, finish that perennial bed, the storm windows and the other things that had been waiting all fall.

"Thought you were staying home this weekend," queried Elizabeth, as she watched me stack the tools. "You know there isn't a chance of a flight this weekend any more than last. The weather report says there will be no change and you know yourself the barometer is steady."

I tried to explain that I had been having a feeling that most barometers couldn't register, a sort of hunch that something might happen which would redeem the past barren month, that to play safe I'd decided to look things over once more, a sort of final reconnaissance, so to speak.

Two hours later, I was in my old blind looking at the same old duckless skyline, watching the slowly drifting haze of forest smoke and a coppery sun working its way over the northern Minnesota wild rice beds. A lone mallard took to the air far down shore, winged its way leisurely toward the horizon. I followed its slow, almost tired flight until it was a mere speck drifting over the trees. For a moment it disappeared and then I saw it again, now steadily holding one position. Suddenly, I realized that it was larger, that it had changed the direction of flight and was coming toward me.

The bird was dropping fast toward the rice bed it had left, then rose once more high above the trees; another low flying circle close to the water and then to my delighted eyes there were two heading swiftly toward my blind. No chance of that pair decoying to a bunch of bluebills off a point. They were looking for some quiet, shallow bay down the lake. There was just a chance, however, that they might come within range.

I slipped off my safety, got set—no use even trying to call that pair—a chance for a double if they were close—hold dead on and pull ahead. Another few seconds and they would be in range. Big birds they were and slow, heavy with the rice they'd been feeding on all fall; not too much of a lead. One was slightly ahead. I held to the point of its bill, followed through and fired, turned quickly and caught the second as it was climbing for the clouds. Both birds were falling now, fell almost together in twin water spouts in the midst of the decoys.

In a moment I had them back in the blind, a greenhead and his mate, laid them close beside me where I could watch the changing colors of their plumage and where I could feel them once in a while just to know my luck had changed. We would have them for Sunday dinner stuffed with wild rice, some cranberries and all the trimmings, concrete evidence of my excellent judgment. I was almost happy as I stood there congratulating myself, almost forgot that my good fortune wasn't due to a shifting of the wind or a change of weather; almost forgot that what I really hoped would happen, that the flight of northern bluebills would somehow get underway, seemed no nearer to materialization.

A raven wheeled high in the still smoky blue, cir-

Mallards taking flight. (Photograph © Bill Marchel)

cling, floating on the light breeze. One wing, I noticed, had lost a feather. It was a rather ragged looking pinion and the bird seemed to favor that side more than the other.

The great bird swung toward me, spiraled sharply downward and lit in a pine tree back of the blind. Then and there it proceeded to tell the world what it thought and watched me with a mind, I was sure, to the potential carrion it hoped I might become. While watching the raven and marveling at the superb scratchiness of its voice, I suddenly became conscious of a difference in the behavior of the blocks. For hours they had bobbed

steadily, sedately, never changing position; but now they were bouncing around frantically, pulling their anchor string, getting together in peculiar and undignified formations; all that, in spite of the fact there had been no apparent change of wind. I had been so busy visiting with the raven that I had failed to notice what was going on, but now I watched the sky, the decoys and the water with new excitement.

Long experience had taught me that decoys can be as good barometers of weather change as the waves themselves. Now they were riding quietly for the first time since I came and the water was dead calm. Then a long series of riffles started out from shore and the rice bent and swayed beyond the decoys, swayed toward the south in a distinct breeze from the hills behind me. In half an hour the air began to clear as the wind out of the north steadied and I knew my hunch had been correct.

At least for the moment, things were different.

If it would only hold, the ducks back in the innumerable pot holes and beaver flowages would get restless and begin to move. I watched those new riffles and prayed. If they stayed, my weekends of waiting would not have been in vain, my sacrifice of the perennials would be more than justified and everything else answered for.

The sky began to darken with real clouds, not smoke this time, and the shores changed from their old sunny gray and red to a somber dullness. The coppery sun disappeared entirely and the air grew appreciably colder. If I were a mallard or even a bluebill, I thought excitedly, and saw what was in the wind, I would pick right up, no matter where I happened to be, and streak straight for the south.

But the mallards did not share my excitement, or the bluebills, and two long hours went by before anything happened. Then came a swift hurricane of wings that almost took my breath away, one closely packed, lonesome bunch of bluebills streaking it down the channel with the speed that only miles of flying can give. Far out of range, the flock bore steadily for the west end of the rice bed with a surety of purpose that bespoke no interest in me, the decoys, or the wonderful stand of rice along my side of the shore. I watched desperately as they grew smaller and smaller, faded at last against the rocks and trees of the far end of the lake. Then, for a panicky moment, I thought I had lost them entirely, that drifting patch of black dots soaring for a moment into the blue only to fuse an instant later with the haze. Then, miracle of miracles, the dots suddenly grew more distinct again, swung swiftly into the wind and came once more down the center of the channel, this time directly toward my point. I crouched, got under cover, prayed with all my soul once more. This was the moment, this the realization of the hunch I had had all week. All I asked was one short chance.

Early Morning Mallards *(1997) by Doug Knutson.*
(Courtesy Apple Creek Publishing)

They were getting larger, swinging toward shore, would surely be in range if they held their present course. Still too high, but as they went over I called steadily, seductively, saw them hesitate, then veer. They had heard and were coming over. This time it would be different.

I shifted my stance, parted the brush in front of me, braced myself in good shooting position, got set.

They were swinging in now, a matter of seconds and they would be in range. Perennials, storm windows, fertilizer and shrubbery, what piddling, mediocre stuff. This was worth dying for.

My safety was off, a new shell in the chamber. A split second and they were in over the decoys—pandemonium—whistling wings—outstretched necks—tails and feet braced for the landing—consternation as I rose.

"Pick your bird and hold dead on; don't shoot at the bunch; always pick a single." The old admonitions flashed into mind. I drew hastily on a big black and white drake, fired and watched with joy as he crumpled neatly and lit. Turning, I drew speedily on another quartering away, saw him skate on the water, bounce with his momentum. And they were gone as swiftly as they had come.

But what was that? A lone single had separated himself from the flock and was tearing back along the shoreline as though possessed. He was coming high, just at the limit of range, would pass right over my point, a perfect overhead shot. Once again, I held at the end of a bill boring into space, this time with a feeling that I could not miss, followed an instant and at the extremity of the angle swept just ahead and fired. At the report, he folded his wings, did a somersault, dove for the rice bed, struck in a funnel of spray. It was the sort of shot one remembers all winter long and I yelled for the sheer joy that was mine. That alone was worth the whole season of waiting, days of standing around with nothing to while away the hours but the chickadees and whiskey jacks, the long empty days with not a wing moving. This was more than compensation, it was double proof that my judgment was infallible.

Pushing the canoe out into the rice, I picked up my ducks almost reverently, two drakes and a hen, all well feathered and plump, the first of the northerns. Back on shore, I hung them carefully in the crotch of an aspen, hung my two mallards just below, admired them to my heart's content. No ordinary birds those, each one a thrilling shot, a story in itself.

I watched the horizon an hour longer, but not another duck swung into view. The shifting of the wind had unsettled one lone flock or perhaps it was just my luck. In any case, the rest of the bluebills knew and to prove that contention, the sun came out once more and the clouds evaporated into the same old hazy sky I had known for a month. Gradually, the wind shifted back to its accustomed corner in the southwest and the flight was over.

Tomorrow, I reflected, was Sunday. Chances were that after this one heaven-sent flurry, nothing would stir for another week. I decided to pick up my outfit, my five beautiful ducks, and go home. In the morning, I thought righteously, I would go to church as a substantial citizen should. I might even get up early and attack that perennial bed or take off the screens. Here was a chance to redeem myself in the eyes of the world.

As I paddled down the lake that afternoon, my mind was at peace and I was happy, happy with the knowledge that I was doing right and that all was well. But at the portage I did an unforgivable thing for a man who has made up his mind. I turned to have one last look at the rice beds against the sunset, stood there athrill with their beauty, watching and wondering. Suddenly against the rosy sky was a long V of black dots and the peace that was mine a moment before vanished swiftly. There must have been 100 and they were settling into the rice near the blind I had left. And there were more, flock after flock in silhouette against the sky. The rice was alive with wings. These ducks, I knew, were riding in ahead of a storm. The flight was on.

For a long time I stood without moving, watched the incoming flocks until it grew too dark to see, wondering what to do. And then I knew, for after all I had promised no one but myself. Almost stealthily, I cached the decoys where I could find them easily in the dark of the morning, threw on the canoe, plodded up the portage toward home.

The end of the day: A hunter picks up decoys. (Photograph © William H. Mullins)

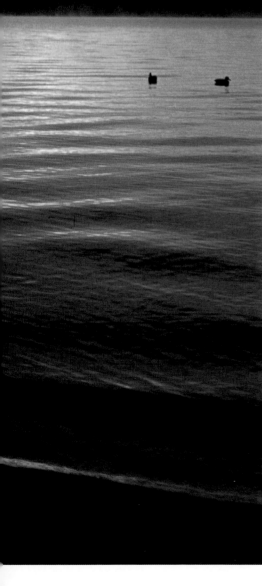

ABOVE: *Chesapeake Bay Premier canvasback decoy from the Mason Decoy Company of Detroit, as well as a reloader, powder and shot dipper, powder can, and paper shells from the early twentieth century. (Photograph © William W. Headrick)*

LEFT: *Watching for ducks at sunrise. (Photograph © Bill Buckley/The Green Agency)*

NOVEMBER WAS ALWAYS THE BEST

By Robert Ruark

Robert Ruark accomplished a great deal during his thirty-year journalistic career, working for major newspapers and as a columnist for the Scripps-Howard Newspaper Alliance and United Features Syndicate. But Ruark was unhappy with his success, and in 1950, he headed for East Africa to pursue big game like his hero, Ernest Hemingway. Though he continued to write for United Features Syndicate, he also wrote about his experiences in Africa, including the books *Horn of the Hunter* (1953), *Something of Value* (1955), and *Uhuru* (1962).

Of course, he later began to write for *Field & Stream*, including his column "The Old Man and the Boy." The autobiographical pieces, inspired by Ruark's childhood relationship with his grandfather, are filled with warmth and wisdom and decency all within a framework of a childhood outdoors.

"November Was Always the Best" first appeared in *Field & Stream* in November 1955 and was later included in the first collection of his columns to be published in book form, *The Old Man and the Boy* (1957).

British Best James Purdey and Sons sidelock ejector built in 1957 for Chicago's Marshall Field store. (Photograph © William W. Headrick)

A LOT OF people figure November to be a middling sad kind of month, with the trees showing naked against the leaden skies late in the afternoon, and the grass all crisp and brown from frost, and the threat of winter turning your ears red in the morning, and the evening cold making your nose run. The year has only one more month to live, and that is sad too, to some people.

But November was the month I aimed my whole year at, for the very simple reason that the bird season opened round about Thanksgiving, and if you lived in my neck of the woods, "birds" didn't mean canaries or parrots or bluejays. Birds meant quail. The Old Man was with me all the way on that one, but he liked to fuzz it up with a little philosophy. Like most pipe smokers, he needed some extras to hang on it to make it dignified.

We were talking about the seasons one time, and the Old Man said that if he had to he could do without summer and all of spring except maybe May, and he would be just as happy to settle for October through January, and give the rest away. He said he would pick November as the best one, because it wasn't too hot, and wasn't too cold, and you could do practically anything in it better than any other time of the year, except maybe get sunburnt or fall in love.

"Although," he said, "there ain't nothing wrong with November, or any other month, for falling in love if the moon's right. But mainly the reason I like November best is that it reminds me of me."

He stopped and struck another kitchen match to his pipe.

"Look at me," he went on. "Here you see a monument to use. I'm too old to fall in love, but I ain't old enough to die. I'm too old to run, but I can outwalk you because I know how to pace myself. I know when to work and when to rest. I know what to eat and what sits heavy on my stomach. I know there ain't any point in trying to drink all the licker in the world, because they'll keep on making it. I know I'll never be rich, but I'll never be stone-poor, neither, and there ain't much I can buy with money that I ain't already got.

"A man don't start to learn until he's about forty; and when he hits fifty, he's learned all he's going to learn. After that he can sort of lay back and enjoy what he's learned, and maybe pass a little bit of it on. His appetites have thinned down, and he's done most of his suffering, and yet he's still got plenty of time to pleasure himself before he peters out entirely. That's why I like November. November is a man past fifty who reckons he'll live to be seventy or so, which is old enough for anybody—which means he'll make it through November and December, with a better-than-average chance of seeing New Year's. Do you see what I'm driving at?"

I said, "Yessir," because I didn't want him to explain it all over again, and because I was worrying about a young pointer puppy who was going to have his first chance at being a working dog, and I was worrying over whether those late rains hadn't drowned off the whole second clutch of quail, and I was worrying over my shooting eye, which had fallen off alarmingly the final two weeks of the last season.

"What's your idea of November?" he asked, his eyes half-closed.

I wanted to tell him that it was mostly the opening of the bird season, and the Thanksgiving holidays, the persimmons wrinkled and ripe on the trees, when the weather was real nice, and it was hog-killing time in the country, and the punkins looked yellow and jolly in the fields, and the sun set good and red, and a lot of other things; but I couldn't manage to squeeze it all out because I had no way with words.

"The bird season," I said.

The Old Man looked at me and sighed. "I reckon I ain't ever going to make no philosopher out of you. Let's us go look at the guns and figger out where we'll best go tomorrow, when she opens."

The day and night before the opening of bird season lasts longer than anything, including the week before Christmas holidays. Awful, horrible thoughts keep you awake, such as will it be raining, or what if the dogs get hot noses or the quail have all moved? And then the next morning dawns clear and bright with just the right breeze, and it is another ten years until afternoon. I used to beg and coax to start in the morning, but the Old Man was stone-set against it.

"There ain't no point to hunting in the morning. Not quail," he said. "They don't feed out until nine or ten o'clock, and later if it's cold, and maybe not at all if it's too hot or raining. And if they come out at all, they

English pointer on point under an overcast sky. (Photograph © Bill Buckley/The Green Agency)

don't go far away from the branches, and they head back before you can get the dogs calmed down. You'll find you'll kill all of your quail in two hours—between three and five o'clock—with very few exceptions. All-day hunting just tires you and the dogs, and if you do get lucky and find birds in the morning you've got your limit and there ain't nothing to do in the afternoon. No, morning is the time for deer and ducks and turkeys, but the bobwhite's a late-sleeping bird."

So we would mess around all morning, and then have us a light lunch about noon. By two o'clock we'd be where we had headed, with the dogs shivering and nipping from excitement and slobbering at the mouth, and me wishing I could. We had a lot of places where

"Designed for adventure," the 1954 Safari hat was a stylish hunting accessory.

we hunted, but we usually started her off at a place called Spring Hill, which we had a lucky feeling for, after trying for three or four coveys closer in, just to let the dogs wet down all the bushes and get the damfoolishness out of their systems.

It is difficult, very hard, to try to explain what a boy feels when he sees the dogs sweeping the browned peafields, or skirting the edges of the gallberry bays, or crisscrossing the fields of yellow withered corn shocks, running like race horses with their heads high and their tails whipping. And then that moment, after nearly a year, of the first dog striking the first scent, and the excitement communicating to the other dogs, and all hands crowding in on the act—the trailers trailing, the winders sniffing high, but slow now, and the final eggshell-creeping, the tails going feverishly and the bellies low to the ground, presaging a point.

Then the sudden freeze, then the slight uncertainty, then a minor change of course, and then the swift, dead-sure cock of head which says plainly the bird is here, boss, right under my nose, and now it's all up to you. The backstanders edge closer, especially the puppy, and the Old Man says sharply, "Whoa!" You walk past the backstanders and then up to the pointer, who is still stamped out of iron, like an animal on a lawn. And you walk past him and kick, but nothing happens.

At this moment a blood-pressure estimate would bust the machine that takes it. Your heart is so loud it sounds like a pile driver. There is something in your throat about the size of a football, and your lips are dry from the temperature you're running, which is maybe just under 110 degrees Fahrenheit. You are looking straight ahead of the dog—never down at the ground—and you are carrying your shotgun slanted across your chest, the stock slightly cocked under your elbow. Nothing happens. The dog changes the position of his head and creeps forward another six yards, and you come up behind him when he freezes again. This time he's looking right down at his forefeet, and when you walk past him he jumps and the world blows up.

The world explodes, and a billion bits of it fly out in front of you, tiny brown bits with the thunder of Jove in each wing. They go in all directions—right, left, behind you, over your head, sometimes straight at you, sometimes straight up before they level. Then a miracle happens.

Bedded quail. (Photograph © Stephen Kirkpatrick)

Out of these billion bits you choose one bit and fire, and if the bit explodes in a cloud of feathers you choose another bit and fire again, and if this bit also explodes you break your gun swiftly and load, figuring maybe there's a lay bird and you can turn to the Old Man with a grin, and when he says, "How many?" you can answer, "Three." More likely you'll answer, "One" or "None."

But the tension is over now, and you find you have broken out into a heavy sweat. If there's a crick nearby, you go and plunge your face in it, or at least you take a long drink from the water bottle. The dogs fetch, and there in your hand is the first bird of the year—the neat, speckled, cockaded little brown fellow with a white chin strap if he's a cock, a yellow necklace if she's hen. He weighs less than half a pound, but has just induced nervous prostration in a man, a boy, and two dogs.

This is when you first sniff the wonderful smell of gunpowder in an autumn wood, and notice that all save the evergreens have crumpled into red and golden and crinkly brown leaves, that the broom grass has gone sere and dusty yellow, and that the sparkleberries are ready to eat, the chinquapins ready to pick. The persimmon tree that always sits lonely at the edge of the cornfield is bare except for the wrinkled yellow balls that the possums love, soft and liver brown-splotched now, and free of the alum that ties your tongue in knots and turns your mouth inside out.

The dogs are roving out ahead, and the Old Man says, "Well, we didn't do so bad for beginners. Anybody here notice where the singles went?"

"I thought about six went over there by that patch of scrub oak, just at the end of the broom," I say.

"Le's go have us a good look," the Old Man suggests. "The dogs seem to think you may be right. Old Frank has either found a friend or turned into a stump."

At the edge of the broom, with the scattered scrub oaks making a screen before the swamp, is old Frank, nailed to something. And over there, like a lemon-spotted statue, is Sandy, nailed to something else.

"You take this 'un, I'll take that 'un," the Old Man says. "We'll walk up together."

Two birds get up under my dog's nose, and I miss both clean, *blim-blam!* I hear the Old Man shoot once, and then the rest of the group explodes in my face, and me with the gun broke and both barrels empty. I load and another bird, a sneaker, gets up behind me, and I whirl and watch him drop off the end of my gun barrel.

"That's enough," the Old Man says. "We got three apiece. Le's go find another covey. There used to be one hell of a big one over the top of that rise that we never had no luck with last year. I was beginning to think they was bewitched when the season ended. Unless the cats and the foxes been at 'em, we could take the rest of the limit out of that 'un and not even make a dent in 'em."

The Old Man lights his pipe and I break an apple out of my pocket. I think I never really appreciated an apple until I ate it in the November woods, after the first covey of the first day of the year. We follow the dogs over the hill; and when we top the brow, there is the white dog stiff, the black dog backing, and the puppy sort of sitting back on his haunches, wondering what to do next.

This didn't happen every day, or even every year, but once in a while it happened like that, and I mean to say that the walk up to where the dogs were painted against the side of a hill was the longest, happiest journey I ever took in my life.

ABOVE: *Ad for the Northwestern School of Taxidermy, Omaha, Nebraska, 1951.*

LEFT: *Hunter and German shorthair in search of game. (Photograph © Bill Buckley/The Green Agency)*

JAKE'S RANGERS HUNT THE WHITETAIL

By Edmund Ware Smith

The Maine wilderness is vast, a seemingly unending forest that would be more appropriate in a place like Alaska than in the upper reaches of populous New England. But Maine has always been a unique place, a land of solitude, true wildness, and few people. It attracted Henry David Thoreau, among other noted writers, and it was the home of and subject matter for Edmund Ware Smith.

Born in Connecticut, Smith became smitten with Maine at a young age and made the state his adopted home. He spent some ten years in a cabin in the wilderness, and wrote often of his hunting and fishing exploits in the woods. Many of his stories were published in *Field & Stream* and *Outdoor Life*, as well as in publications for the Ford Motor Company, and he also wrote several books, including *A Tomato Can Chronicle, and Other Stories of Fishing and Shooting* (1937), *Tall Tales and Short* (1938), *The One-Eyed Poacher of Privilege* (1941), and *A Treasury of the Maine Woods* (1958).

"Jake's Rangers Hunt the Whitetail" was first published in *Field & Stream* in October 1959 and later appeared in *Upriver and Down* (1965), a collection of Smith's greatest hunting and fishing tales.

Fog enshrouds a whitetail buck. (Photograph © Alan and Sandy Carey)

Whether you call them "The Trail Blazers," or "Whitetails Limited," or simply "The Old Bunch," it means the same thing when the leaves begin to fall in the little towns in the deer-hunting states of our nation. Whatever the name, and there usually is one, you are talking about a group of men, young and old, who gather each fall to hunt the whitetail deer.

The personnel of these groups is often so varied in age and walk of life that individual members rarely meet during the rest of the year. But with the first frost, and the foliage bright on the ridges, there comes a flurry of eager telephone calls. Meetings are held, the trip is planned; and, when you reach your hunting camp, you are reunited like brothers. Your rifle stands in the gun rack where it stood last year. Your sleeping bag is on your old bunk or bed. You are fraternal in the glow of lamplight, sharing the familiar warmth of the wood stove with the old bunch, and talking of just one subject—tomorrow. For tomorrow is opening day on deer.

Each fall, the phenomenon of the deer-hunting groups grows deeper into the country's grass roots. In Pennsylvania, New York, the Virginias, the Carolinas, Michigan, Maine, and perhaps other states, there are groups that were first organized well over fifty years ago. Rich in tradition, and sometimes in ritual, this annual gathering of the deer-hunting clan has become an American institution.

I suspect that my own bunch is typical of at least a hundred others. We call ourselves "Jake's Rangers"; and, in this description of the Rangers' fourteenth annual hunt, I believe you will find striking similarities to your own hunt, and perhaps a kinship between your group and ours. In fact, in what follows, you may even read words that you have actually spoken or heard spoken at night around the stove in your own hunting camp. For example:

"I was standing in a little spruce knoll, when I heard this deer coming."

That opening line, with minor variations, has been uttered at least once for every whitetail deer sighted, heard, hit or missed, since deer hunting began. It can't be copyrighted, for it is always an inspired original to the hunter who is telling his story. Certain of Jake's Rangers will be speaking the magic line presently, but first I must explain who we are and where we hunt.

Officially, there are seven Rangers. Guests bring the total to ten or more. All of us reside in, or near, the small seacoast town of Damariscotta, Maine. Typically heterogeneous, our membership includes Damariscotta's postmaster, its veterinary surgeon, its Railway Express agent, a leading physician, an insurance man, a cabinet maker, a grocer, and an artist. We have named ourselves for our leader, Maurice "Jake" Day, known to his Rangers as "the Colonel." To the rest of the world, he is Maurice Day, artist, naturalist, and authority on the woods and waters of the Pine Tree State. His nationally known watercolors of wilderness Maine are considered important regional documents, and in many of them, his favorite wild animal appears. Appropriately, it's the whitetail deer.

Every group of hunters, by tradition, has to have an old-timer, a colorful character, or highly developed curmudgeon, who is an unfailing source of camp anecdote and humor. Our candidate in this field—the man who sets Jake's Rangers apart from all other groups—is Uncle George Whitehouse, age seventy-four.

Uncle George, who used to be a boat builder and almost everything else, weighs in at around a hundred and six pounds. In build, he is virtually one-dimensional—like a canoe pole. Despite the spareness of his frame, his feats of strength and conquests of all types, as reported by himself, are without equal. He has rigged more topmasts on more four-masted schooners, felled more trees, shot more and bigger deer at greater distances, and run wilder rapids in smaller canoes—or just on logs—than any man alive. He doubts nothing that he says. His chief characteristic is his halo of invincibility.

Jake's Rangers regard Uncle George as an endowment. He is in residence the year-round in the deer-hunting camp at Sprague's Falls on the Narraguagus River, near Cherryfield in Washington County. This is fortunate, because when the camp—an old farmhouse—showed signs of sagging at the sills, it was nothing for Uncle George, alone, to hold the building off the ground with one hand while he shored it up with the other.

Annually, before departing for camp and Uncle George, the Rangers go through a stage of high-octane anticipation. It has become a kind of ritual: listing and packing supplies, sighting in rifles at the local rifle range,

An early-winter hunter heads afield. (Photograph © Bill Marchel)

airing sleeping bags, applying the whetstone to hunting knives, switching from white handkerchiefs to red ones.

Bentley Glidden, Damariscotta's postmaster, invariably squeezes rare juices of drama from these preliminaries. He telephones his fellow Rangers at odd hours. You pick up the receiver. A sepulchral voice comes over the wire:

"Is your waterproof match safe full?" Or, "Have you remembered your compass?" Or, "Only you can prevent forest fires."

Bentley is a rotund, merry, and uninhibited organizer. If you step into his Post Office in mid-October,

with the opening of deer season still two weeks hence, your name is sure to be called loudly and jubilantly. Bent will snatch you into his back room, and read you the camp menu for the entire ten days:

"Friday, first night in camp: hamburg, onions, mashed potato. Saturday, opening-day night: deer liver (?) and bacon, or baked beans."

Sometimes, without a word, Bent will hand you a slip of paper, turn his back on you, and disappear into the darker confines of the Post Office. This year I got the paper treatment twice. The first listed the personnel of the trip as follows:

Jake (our leader), Mac (McClure Day, our veterinary surgeon, who is Jake's son), Eddie Pierce (who owns Damariscotta's Yellow Front Grocery), Dr. Sam Belknap (The Rangers' physician), Jack (Bentley's brother, our insurance man), Bud Hauglund (Railway Express agent, a newcomer), Louis Doe (Mayor of the nearby village of Sheepscott), Ed Smith (yours truly), and Bentley Glidden.

The explanatory parentheses are mine. The final words addressed to me, are Bentley's. They follow:

Please remember that you were inducted into Jake's Rangers during "Be Kind to Animals Week."

The second paper that Bentley slipped me was a command that I obeyed with pleasure. It read:

Have your station wagon in the alley back of Eddie Pierce's store at three-thirty, Thursday, October 30.
    [Signed] Sgt. B. Glidden, Jake's Rangers.

The loading of grub and supplies in Eddie Pierce's back alley is always a ceremony. It's the last act in Bentley's anticipation byplay and is attended by all Rangers able to sneak a few minutes off from work. Bentley had read the camp menu to all of us, and now—passing carton by carton over the tail gate of my wagon—was the reality: a colossal turkey, an Olympian ham, a classic corned-beef brisket, enough hamburg to equip a diner, bacon, flour, canned fruits, juices, vegetables.

As the last parcel was loaded, a bystander remarked with heavy sarcasm:

"You poor guys are going to starve up there in the woods."

"Oh, no," said Bent, airily, "we'll eke this out with venison and partridge."

I locked the tail gate carefully over all this bounty, drove home, and locked the wagon in my barn as a double security measure. I was to pick up Bentley at daylight, and we were to drive to camp ahead of the others in order to make things ready and establish peace with Uncle George.

We had had five straight days of rain, but Friday morning was as clear as a bell, with mist veils hanging low in the valleys, and the color of the last, lingering foliage painting the ridges in the sunrise.

Camden, Belfast, Bucksport, Ellsworth. The white towns flashed by, and everywhere you could see signs announcing: "Hunters' Breakfast—4 A.M. to 8 A.M." We saw other hunters heading toward their camps. Tomorrow, November first, was opening day, and the deer-hunting clans were on their way to rendezvous.

Beyond Ellsworth, the road traversed the shore of Tunk Lake, with Tunk Mountain to the north. Then the magic turnoff toward Sprague's Falls, the end of blacktop, then narrow, rutted gravel. Jake's Rangers' headquarters is the last farmhouse at the dead end of the Sprague Falls Road. There, Uncle George, in his tattered checked shirt, greeted us from thirty feet in the air. He was prancing along the ridgepole of the house, where he had been examining a chimney for smoke leaks. I held my breath while Uncle George, all the time waving at us, danced down an intricate system of ladders to the ground.

"I was scared you'd fall, Uncle George," I said.

"Five, ten years ago," he said, "I'd of jumped. Once, in a shipyard in East Boothbay, I jumped sixty feet from the topmast of a—"

"Never mind, Uncle George," Bentley said. "How's the firewood supply?"

Uncle George gave Bent an outraged look.

"Firewood? When that chimney might leak flame? Burn us all to a cinder? Would *you* of cut any?"

Uncle George was in splendid form. So was the chimney. And I had a newly filed bucksaw and an axe in the wagon. While we unloaded the supplies, Uncle George told of new enemies he had made during the past months and of his plans for disposing of them. He had done in quite a few of them, when Bentley interrupted with The Great Hardy Perennial Hunters' Question:

"Are there many deer around, Uncle George?"

"Not a one. No deer at all."

Bent and I looked at each other in a flood of relief. Uncle George's reply was a surefire omen that whitetails were plentiful. So eager were we to relay the glad tidings that we could hardly wait for the arrival of the rest of the Rangers. But the time went fast, and with the thunder of Sprague's Falls familiar in our ears, we went to work cutting wood, policing camp, and stacking supplies on the shelves.

The smell of your hunting camp, as you step across

the threshold for the first time in a year, is as familiar as the palm of your hand. There's the smoke of old fires, oilcloth, coffee, kerosene, soap, gun oil, cedar kindling, and, on rainy days, the steam of damp wool and leather and rubber.

That first noon, while we were eating the lunch our wives had prepared for us at home, Bent and I noticed a new, strange odor in camp. Uncle George had loftily disdained to share our lunch and, instead, opened the door to his iceless, wooden, icebox. The box contained nothing save a fragment of dried pollock, and the new scent emanated from the pollock. I don't know how long Uncle George had been nourishing himself from this item, but it had a perfume definitely redolent of an old Model pollock. The old-timer shaved off a portion with his jackknife, chewed it with relish, and closed the icebox door, lest the remainder escape under its own power. The scent of mink bait vanished with the closing of the box, and we were at peace again—until Uncle George fired us up with the one, burning rumor that can galvanize any hunting camp.

"I hear," he said, "that there's a white buck around."

Even if the rumor was one of Uncle George's invention, the Rangers' hunt was made. All of us would be buoyant with the individual dream of at least a running shot at the white buck.

Jake Day and Mac drove into the dooryard at midafternoon. Before they had their rifles in the rack, Bent had told them of the rumored prize. They asked Uncle George if he had seen the great white creature.

At the outset, Uncle George had just heard. Now, it developed, he had seen.

"How many points?" asked Jake.

"Where was he?" asked Mac.

Uncle George waved a hand toward the wilderness stretching

Bushnell Scopes ad, 1954.

northward. His gesture was wide enough to include Tunk, Bog, McCabe, and Spring River Mountains, together with a fifty-degree segment of the Great Barrens—in all, roughly seventy square miles.

"Right there," said Uncle George, "is where I saw him."

By the time Jack Glidden, Eddie Pierce, Dr. Sam, and Bud Haugland arrived, it was dark. The night was still, except for the hollow rumble of Sprague's Falls—a sound that is built into the rafters of the old house. In a matter of a few hours, the white buck had ceased being a rumor. He was real. He was somewhere. He was everyone's goal, the substance of everyone's wakeful dreams that first night in camp.

Which rifle in the full gun rack would have the honor? Would any of them? I lay in my sleeping bag, wondering and visualizing the gleaming barrels. Most of the guns had names: "Cosmic Ray," a couple of "Betsys," and "Old Meat in the Pot"—and then there was Mac Day's .243, which came to be known as "Little Evil."

Bent and I cooked opening-day breakfast by

lamplight, while, by custom, Dr. Sam made the toast and prepared the noonday sandwiches with his camp buddy, Eddie Pierce.

"Where you going to hunt today?"

That's the breakfast question. You hear it a dozen times every morning for the hunt's duration. A good question. If you know where your people are working, you avoid accidents. If a man gets lost, you know where to start looking.

Bent and Jack Glidden headed for the "Bowl," Bud for the "River Trail," Dr. Sam and Eddie for "Split Rock." These are landmark names first coined by Jake's Rangers. They are not on any map but our own. Other hunters range the same places, knowing them by different names.

Jake, Mac, and I took our rifles from the rack, crossed the decaying wooden bridge at the Falls, and started out toward the Barrens. This vast, boulder-strewn area is grown to scrub oak, small beech, and other hardwoods, with occasional "islands" of spruce and fir. Its high plateau fans off for miles. In the past, millions of feet of pine logs have been harvested from this reach and, latterly, millions of bushels of blueberries. An ancient tote road makes the gradual ascent to the plateau.

Mac left us and struck out alone into the woods to the westward. We watched him go. You could see his red shirt and cap, and the yellow glow of his *Fire-Glo* vest. You saw a good woodsman in action—hand instinctively fending the sharp twig and eyes focused yards ahead, channeling the way the foot would travel, estimating the slant of ledge or boulder, testing by sight and memory the traction of the trail, and the rifle— Little Evil—cradled in his elbow, a part of the man. It has a peculiar grace and is a nice thing to see.

When Jake and I reached the Barrens, the wind had picked up to a half-gale. We heard voices, and a group of four hunters emerged from a thicket—three boys, and an older man who bore the stamp of experience. His name was Grant, and he told us they hadn't seen even a track since daylight. The younger boys looked discouraged. They were pulling out for new territory.

When they had gone, Jake and I sat behind a huge boulder, out of the chill wind. Jake told of his experi-

Copper sunlight, autumn fields, and a whitetail buck. (Photograph © Bill Marchel) ence of the previous year—how he was walking along the Barrens' trail and a buck crossed ten yards in front of him, how he put his rifle to his shoulder, and then how a partridge boomed right up into his face between him and the deer.

"That buck should have credited the partridge with an assist," Jake said—and then we heard a shot.

Shots always fill you full of excited speculations. They have tremendous mystery—even the far ones that sound like someone whispering "Pow" in your ear. Each one can mean drama or climax or both. The shot we'd just heard sounded sharp, and there wasn't a second shot. Just that single, powerful, "Cr-rack!"

"That could be Mac and Little Evil," I said.

Jake was on his feet, and we hurried off down the trail over which we'd just come. Two minutes later, we froze in our tracks. Three or four rifles were blazing away. You couldn't count the shots. You could tell the "Bat-bat-bat—" of an automatic. The slower cadence of a lever action. Then came silence, except for the wind hollering in our ears.

We went on cautiously around a couple of bends in the trail. Ahead of us, standing in a group, we saw six hunters. Two of them were Mac Day and Dr. Sam Belknap; the other four were the Grant party—the discouraged ones. But they weren't discouraged now. They were dressing out a handsome doe. Mac had sighted the doe, and his shot had driven the animal up to the Grant boys.

When Jake and I joined the group, the tall Grant brother—the experienced one—was giving his boys a stern lecture on too much shooting. You couldn't blame the kids for their excitement. But it was a sound lecture, just the same.

"We had the doe after the first shot," said the older Grant. "All the other shots did was ruin good meat. You kids think of that, next time. You want to have some respect for your deer."

That was a good speech, and as we started back toward camp, I thought how those boys would remember it, and someday tell their own boys the same thing.

None of the other Rangers were at camp when Jake and I got back. But Uncle George was there, and he was in a cold, trembling fury, his eyes flaming like a blowtorch. The object of his wrath was a group of Connecticut hunters who had just parked their car in our dooryard and were standing around it with their rifles. Our dooryard is the customary parking place for hunters in this vicinity, simply because there is no other place. Uncle George now stated that they ought to pay a parking fee, and that the Connecticut hunters owed him for two years, besides this one. He would take it out of their hides.

We watched while Uncle George, picking up a stout cudgel, went out to assault the army from Connecticut. This is what we saw:

Uncle George crossing the yard to the car under the apple tree, eagerly and companionably shaking hands with all four hunters; smiles of welcome and goodwill on all faces; a tall, red-coated Connecticut man handing Uncle George a bill; Uncle George waving the billed hand away in austere refusal.

And then we heard Uncle George say:

"You boys park here any time you want, day or night. Always glad to see you coming back."

I don't know whether it's more fun to hunt the daylight hours to the full or to spend an afternoon in camp looking up the trail, watching the Rangers come in one by one or two by two, and listening to their individual stories as they arrive at the door, unload their rifles, place them in the gun rack, take off their wet boots, and stretch their weary feet toward the fireplace fire. But this first afternoon after Jake and Mac left for The Big Pine, I decided to stay in and nurse a toe blister.

Bud Haugland came in about three o'clock.

"Any excitement, Bud?"

Bud grinned.

"An open, running shot—not twenty yards away. It was just now, a couple of hundred yards from camp."

"I didn't hear the shot—and I've been listening hard."

"There wasn't any shot," Bud said. "The safety was on."

The shadows got long. Bud cleaned lamp chimneys and filled lamps. Together we worked up a woodpile and stacked it on the back porch.

Mac and Jake came in. No story. Dr. Sam and Eddie Pierce came in. No story.

"You boys don't seem to be very good hunters,"

An early Griffen and Howe 7x57 rifle with Lyman Alaskan scope. (Photograph © William W. Headrick)

ABOVE: The Hunter *(1932) by Oliver Kemp.*

FACING PAGE: *New snow fronts the ground and the back of this whitetail buck. (Photograph © Doug Locke)*

remarked Uncle George. "I always had my buck—a big one—hung up before seven o'clock in the morning on opening day. Sixty years running."

Bud got up and lighted the big lamp over the dining table. It was twilight outside, with full dark beginning to hover down. There was that moment of anxiety so well known to any hunting camp, that strange dread of a hunter lost, of darkness. Two men were missing.

"Where did Bentley and Jack go?" Jake asked.

"The Bowl," said Dr. Sam, who has a way of keeping track of such things.

"Maybe they got on the white buck's track," Eddie said. "That could keep them out late."

Jake began to pace up and down in front of the fireplace. Mac looked at his compass and at the framed map on the long table.

Then came the familiar voices just outside the front door. There also came a heavy thud, a groan—as in relief at dropping a heavy burden after a long, rugged

haul. We grabbed flashlights and rushed outside. Bentley and Jack, their backs steaming in the chill air, stood beside the eight-pointer they had shot on the edge of the Bowl and lugged in over that rough terrain on a pole. First buck! First blood! Opening day.

"I was sitting there on a stump," said Bentley, "and Jack sitting right near me, when I saw this deer come sneaking along."

Both the boys had fired. Both had connected. The buck had dropped instantly. Supper that night was liver and bacon.

The things you remember about the days and nights in camp—the things that keep coming back! The sounds of going to bed, the bunk springs twanging, the boots thudding on the floor; the penny-ante poker game with Uncle George standing by, telling of the times he had risked a thousand dollars on a single turn of a card; the chain-reaction coffee that Jack Glidden made; the day Bentley saw the black bear; the reshuffling of the

Deer hunter at sunrise. (Photograph © Ron Spomer)

contents of duffle bags, choosing the proper clothes against the probabilities of weather; the Sundays in camp—no hunting, but visiting with other hunters. And had anyone caught a glimpse of the white buck?

One afternoon it rained hard. That morning Uncle George had told me of two mongrel dogs belonging to a neighbor, and how he planned to do away with them. They stole his food, he said, which was why he kept his dried pollock in the iceless icebox. He had decided to pinch off the animals' heads with his own hands, but only after inflicting tortures of a surgical nature.

When the rain started that afternoon, and I came back from limiting the river, I stepped into the clearing and saw Uncle George and the dogs on the back steps. He was feeding the creatures choice scraps and speaking to them in words of endearment, all the while fondling their ears. To save Uncle George the shame and guilt of being caught red-handed in an act of tenderness, I remained hidden till the scene broke up.

That was the afternoon that Jake tagged an eight pointer in the rain. He and Mac lugged it in and hung it alongside the Glidden boys' in the cellar under the farmhouse. It was a perfect mate for Jack's and Bentley's.

"I had just stepped over a little knoll," said Jake, "and I heard this noise, and I stopped still, and—"

A clean shot high on the backbone. No spoilage.

Through the years, Jake's Rangers have had a high of nine deer, which was one apiece for that year. The low was three. This trip was about average, with a total of four. Dr. Sam tagged a fat and highly edible spikehorn near Wasse's Beaver dam on about the fifth or sixth day.

I remember it was the day I left camp late in the morning, because I saw the Rural Delivery mailman stop at Uncle George's mailbox—the last mailbox on the Sprague Falls Road. Uncle George sprang hopefully from the front door and opened the box. Whatever was in it was for the Smith Camp across the river. The old-timer shook his head dejectedly.

"Nothing for me again," he said.

"Were you expecting a letter?" I asked.

"It's a long time," he said, with a sigh, "since I've heard from Theda Bara."

Jake's Rangers are a bunch of hardworking, re-

sourceful hunters, and most of them are on the go from daylight till dark. I am content with a few hours. Maybe it's middle age, or a slight lameness in my back. Or maybe it's just that I can get as big a heart bump out of someone else shooting a deer as if I did it myself. That's probably a false statement, but on this particular day it wasn't.

Mac Day and Jake came in from their hunting on "The Mountain," a wild, rocky nubble on the west side of the river. Excitement was all over them like flame, and it caught me in its contagion. Mac drew his hunting knife and showed the blade. It had a yellow-white coating.

"What's that, Mac?"

"It's not candle wax!"

"You got the white buck!"

"Yes—me and Little Evil. We need help hauling him in."

Western Hunter Company Deer Bag ad, 1945.

Then Mac told it. He had been catfooting near the top of the mountain, Jake right behind him with his camera. He had stepped up on a rock, and there in a little draw, not sixty feet away, stood the white buck. The deer dropped with Mac's first shot, lifted its head once, then slowly sank back, still.

It turned out that the famous buck wasn't pure white, but calico. But it was an experience Mac and Jake will never forget, nor will I as I saw and heard them tell the story. As I write this, soon after the Rangers' return home, the four deer are hanging in the big, walk-in freezer in Eddie Pierce's grocery store. Hometown people go in for a look now and then, and anytime you happen to meet Jake, or Jack, or Bentley, or Dr. Sam, or Mac on Main Street, you can ask for the story, and it will begin with minor variations of deer hunting's immortal, and forever original opening line:

"I was standing on a little spruce knoll, when I heard this deer coming."

As for Uncle George Whitehouse, I feel it just and proper that he should have the last word. There is a moment of something like sadness when you stand at the camp door and say good-by for a year. It was particularly so when I said good-by to Uncle George. As I looked around over the land and forest, I thought of the snow that would come inevitably, the road closed in drifts that would cover the mailbox, the smoke from the chimney lonely and torn in the winter wind, and the old man huddled by the fire.

"Are you going to winter here?" I asked, as we shook hands.

"No," said Uncle George, nibbling the last of his dried pollock, "I've been thinking some of the French Riviera."

ABOVE: *A 1950s postcard.*

FACING PAGE: *A regal whitetail on the edge of a pine forest. (Photograph © Stephen Kirkpatrick)*

WHEN A MAN'S THOUGHTS ARE PURE

By Havilah Babcock

Havilah Babcock was a southern gentleman, born and raised in South Carolina. He was on the English faculty of the University of South Carolina at Charleston for most of his working life, rising to head of the department in 1939. He was also a prolific writer and dedicated hunter, contributing more than one hundred articles about his days afield to national magazines such as *Field & Stream*, and writing seven books, including *My Health Is Better In November* (1947), *Tales of Quail 'n' Such* (1951), and *I Don't Want To Shoot an Elephant* (1958).

"When a Man's Thoughts Are Pure" first appeared in the December 1964 issue of *Field & Stream*. Babcock died shortly after its publication.

A lone waterfowler paddles to his blind, 1967. (Photograph courtesy State Historical Society of Wisconsin)

MY DIVERSIONS ARE hunting, fishing, and vegetable gardening, and teaching is my trade. How, I often ask, could a man be divided up more pleasantly? Teaching has brought me so much pleasure that I could list it as a pastime too. I may not have everything I want, but what I haven't got I can do without, which makes me rich. I don't covet my neighbor's maidservant, his ox, nor yet his ass.

I have been hunting and fishing most of my remembering days, and I enjoy these diversions as much now as ever. But as a man grows older his concept of a good time changes. So does his idea about what constitutes a successful hunting or fishing trip. When I was younger the measure of success was what I brought back.

I still like to bring home something to grace the dinner table when I go hunting or fishing, and I can imagine no finer reason for going. The world was made to be lived in as well as looked at, and nature's supermarket is well stocked if you don't mind its self-service feature.

But the size of the bag is no longer the sole criterion. I find, as I acknowledge the passing years, that the incidental gains—fringe benefits, they are called nowadays—are becoming more important, and I am growing more aware of the little extras that set a day apart and make the memory of it more fragrant.

But what brings pleasure to one may bring displeasure to another. Whenever I go for a day's hunting I like to get up an hour or so be-sun, to use a grandfatherly phrase. And I like to bustle around the kitchen and get my own breakfast. There is a sort of chumminess about a well-ordered kitchen at 4 in the morning, its full-bodied aromas and bubbly breakfast noises putting one in a mellow mood for the day.

But Alice sees no point in parting company with her bed in the stilly night, nor does she share my interest in daybreaks, a subject about which I am supposed to be something of a nut. The breaking of day is for me a quiet miracle, bringing balm to hurt spirits and a moment of privacy in which to contemplate the day ahead. Forever old and forever new, a sunrise is always and never the same.

Alice enjoys telling people that I go into the yard every morning and help the day to break. She also ac-

cuses me of hunting and fishing as an excuse for getting up early, to keep the neighbors from thinking I'm a pagan sunworshiper or crackpot.

When I go for a day's hunt in my beloved low country, I get up in what Alice unpoetically calls the middle of the night, drive seventy-five miles, sit in my car and talk about bird hunting with a crony while waiting for the darkness to lift from the fields and woods around me, and consider the whole thing a bargain. And while waiting I enjoy socializing a bit with my dogs in the trunk of the car.

"Fleet, how are you doing back there, old lady?" I might call out, and a thumping tail would be sure to answer.

"And you, Sambo, what have you got to say for yourself?" Another answering thump, and I know I am among friends.

It has often occurred to me that women should encourage their husbands to hunt and fish, because such activities help to keep them out of mischief. After all, a man can chase only one thing at a time, and his thoughts are pretty likely to be pure when he is netting a fish, unraveling a backlash, disentangling a monofilament line from a brush pile on a windy day, or looking for a dog on point.

Women whose husbands hunt and fish derive another fringe benefit: they get the menfolk out of their hair. However indispensable a man may be, and however multifarious his uses around the house, there are times when he is a fly in the ointment, a drug on the market, and a plain superfluity. There should be a law requiring every husband to stay away from home two nights a month so his wife can exercise her inalienable right to move the furniture, to let the dishes lie unchastened in the sink, and to be unglamorous.

Husbands may turn such temporary sundering of bed-and-board to their advantage too if they time their return right. Knowing when to come back is just as important as knowing when to leave. Getting back from a hunting or fishing trip on time is the biggest mistake a man can make. He should always stay late enough for his wife to worry about him, past the "Where-in-the-hell-have-you-been?" stage and well into the "Thank-God-you're-back" stage.

I have often said that the bobwhite is America's

Hunter and hound pause for a scratch between the ears. (Photograph © Bill Buckley/The Green Agency)

most superb game bird, and that the pursuit of this gallant little fellow is the pastime of a scholar and a gentleman. I may not fit either of these categories, but few men have pursued *Colinus virginianus* longer or more ardently than I, yet I am sometimes baffled by his quirks and whimsies. Where, for instance, does he go when he isn't there? How does he manage at times— even in territory where he is known to exist in great plenitude—to be completely unfindable?

There are days, indeed, when a poor, disheartened hunter might almost conclude the species has become extinct, as with head bowed and spirits adroop he homeward plods his weary way. But what is this his sharp eye catches which quickly assures him that the species is not extinct, and that a sizable bevy was in recent occupancy and may even now be in the environs? Nothing other than a quail roost.

Such a roost is always an object of interest and curiosity to me. The pattern of droppings is distinctive and unique, and the bedding habit of quail is evidence of the innate cunning of the wild. Perhaps his manner of roosting is one way of coping with his enemies. Groundling that he is, Bob must be prepared from darkness to dawn for sudden alarms and instant flight. Only through the alertness of every member of a covey can it be forewarned of lurking peril. Such alertness is achieved by roosting in a complete circle, with tails in the center and heads turned outward to spy out danger.

And a tight circle it is. On frosty mornings quail are inclined to lie abed, and I have seen a bevy of fifteen in a knot that the crown of my hat would have covered. No wonder a covey seems to explode when startled! But I have never seen birds collide on takeoff, each being a missile aimed along its own path.

The close circle also imprisons the scent arising from the family discharge. If uncurbed, such effluvium might prove a fatal giveaway to nocturnal marauders. I have often suspected that quiescent animals have some unexplored ability for withholding body scent, that something beyond mere immobility is involved. Certainly a dog may pass within two feet of a bedding covey without detecting its presence.

Pointers on the edge of a cornfield. (Photograph © Bill Buckley/The Green Agency)

Krieghoff K-80 over-under shotgun and sporting pins. (Photograph © Dale C. Spartas/The Green Agency)

An experienced observer can estimate the size of a bevy by its roost, but a companion of mine who fancies himself an expert in this field of deduction once allowed himself to fall into a trap. Or more accurately, he was pushed into it. The owner of a commercial quail hatchery had brought me a bag of quail manure for my vegetable garden, and when I looked at the great profusion of "sign" a malicious idea popped into my head.

The following day I sneaked off to a swamp where we sometime hunted, and where my companion had called attention to a cluster of roosts. When I left, there reposed on what poets call the forest floor a quail roost such as no mortal eye had ever beheld. The next day

my companion, with a little maneuvering on my part, discovered the planted evidence, and his voice boomed through the woods.

"Great balls of fire! Come here quick!" Down on his knees, he was pointing dramatically at the wondrous pyramid. "Have you ever in all your born days?"

"How many would you say?" I prodded, helping him admire the phenomenon.

My companion picked up a stick to aid his calculations, but withheld his hand from demolishing so wondrous an edifice. "I'm coming back with my camera," he explained.

Then, with the half-closed eyes of a connoisseur

appraising a chef-d'oeuvre, he surveyed the miniature pyramid from different angles and awesomely intoned, "I'd give it as my considered opinion that this covey had in the neighborhood of 150 birds!"

But in a moment he recovered from his trance, jumped up and sputtered, "Goshamighty: That's impossible!"

Throughout the afternoon he shook his head in puzzlement and mumbled unhappily to himself. I hope it is needless to say that I never confessed the swindle. But my companion got his revenge without being aware of it: for three days straight he dragged my unhappy carcass through that swamp in quest of the phantom covey.

Another sure sign that "Kilroy was here," and one which always brings me quiet pleasure to come upon, is a bevy's "wash," or dust bath. In loose woods earth on the sunny side of logs such curiosities are most likely to be found. They interest me not only because they advertise the presence of birds in the neighborhood but because I carry a mental picture of what happens in such communal baths.

I have lain in the brush and watched an entire bevy, one after another in orderly fashion, perform its fluttery ablutions. I have seen them stand in a sort of anteroom, busying themselves with idle chatter, while waiting their turn for the shower; and once inside, each bather disported himself with such spirit that its small body was almost swallowed in a miniature dust cloud. Although birds appear to enjoy the exercise, dust-bathing is a cleansing rite rather than an idle sport. As all observing hunters know, birds engage in such "washing" to suffocate the lice and other mites on their bodies.

What is more beautiful than a pointing dog? And what hunter is so impassive that he can contemplate one without a quickening of pulses and a surging of hope? "Statuesque," a pointing dog is often called, but no statue, however exquisite, can hold a candle to the real thing. I would like my dog to point with head and tail aloft, to be the fashion plate that finicky field-trial judges demand that he be. But if he didn't point like an all-time champion, even if he dropped to the ground and bellied forward like a base-born cur, I would forgive him and he would still be my dog, because that

was the kind I hunted with when I was a boy. My first dogs were all groundlings and "pumpers," as we called them, and great self advertisers.

I could hear one pumping up the ground fifty yards away, but if there was a covey in that end of the county, and I didn't run out of time, he would find it. In dry weather such a dog was a godsend, picking up and working a trail that an air-minded aristocrat would have missed or disdained to follow. Truth to tell, with quail becoming denizens of the deep-tangled wildwood in many areas, such a dog might be a godsend today.

When old Boss, the brag dog of my boyhood, finally snorted and pumped his way to the environs of a covey, he would flop down and begin praying. The nearer he got, the more he debased himself, dragging his carcass along the ground as if every movement would be his last. And on every covey rise old Boss had a nervous breakdown. So did I; how I ever got my growth I don't know.

Even now a dog that bellies down and goes into histrionics on point sends my blood pressure away up. But there is a thing or two to be said for such earthlings. Certainly they prolong the agony and the ecstasy longer than dogs that race up and slam on the brakes, although this may not be a favor. And in defense of trailing it might be argued that Bob belongs to the infantry, too, traveling mostly afoot, and that ground scent is the basis of bird hunting. I am in favor of any dog that will find and hold a bird until I get there. If he looks like Abercrombie & Fitch, fine and dandy; but if he is a lazy homespun character that points with his tail at half-mast, at least he points. After all, what makes a dog a bird dog is what he does about birds.

"How does a bird dog's sense of smell compare with that of other hunting dogs?" I am sometimes asked. Having hunted birds all my life, and nothing but birds, I have no basis for comparison. But two peculiarities have long puzzled me. First, how a dog's acuteness of smell can vary so much—from detecting the presence of birds fifty feet away to being blithely unaware of a skulker under his very nose. Second, how does a dog distinguish the direction from which birds have come from the direction in which they have gone? A good dog will infallibly trail *toward* birds rather than away from them.

A covey's daily neighborhood meanderings might embrace half a mile, and over a variegated terrain, yet a dog can intersect the trail at almost any point and without apparent effort make the right turn. I have often heard dogs accused of backtrailing, but I have seen this happen only a few times, and almost never by a first-class dog.

"Sometime a dog will backtrack on purpose," a shooting companion once told me. "When I was a boy I was a great possum hunter, and I often bragged that Jumbo, my possum dog, never backtracked. But one night Jumbo got chewed up by a ferocious bull possum that had moved into our woods. And for a solid month—until the old boy recovered his nerve—Jumbo backtrailed that big possum every time we went hunting. And with a hurrah that echoed through the hills! Yes, sir," laughed my companion, "Jumbo became an expert on where that possum had been, and not once did he make the mistake of trailing in the right direction!"

One day last season while dawdling over my noonday snack I chanced to see a bevy of quail scurrying across the path ahead. Such a sight would ordinarily have galvanized me into motion, but not that day. Having within one bird of my requirements, and being of a mind to humor my legs a bit and perchance catch a little shuteye, I merely grinned and leaned back against a friendly stump.

An hour or so later I released my dogs from the car and watched with more than passing interest as they picked up the trail and unerringly set off in the right direction. Not a moment's hesitation, no awareness of having solved a problem.

Does the explanation lie in some subtle exhalation from the birds themselves, or in some uncatalogued sense that nature installed in dogs? I suppose there is no percentage in pondering the imponderable. Having been a guest of nature off and on for forty years, I have come to one conclusion: whoever put things on this earth of ours and started them off evidently knew what he was doing.

No dissertation on the pleasures of hunting and fishing should leave out the titillating effects of good conversation. A great beguiler of time and abridger of distances is conversation, for what so shortens a trip as good talk? The charm of good conversation lies in its spontaneity and disrespectfulness, the way it rambles without apology from one topic to another. Lay down rules for the conduct of a conversation and you wind up with a conference, which is a swapping of ignorance and an exercise in mutual boredom. The first requirement of good conversation is that nobody should know what is coming next. Good conversation, of course, demands good companionship. A man may work alone, but it is improbable that he will get much playing done without the companionship of others. Bird hunting is one such social pastime. Companionship is, in fact, half the hunt and may go far toward redeeming a bad day. Certainly it should be listed among the pleasures of hunting, but tastes in companionship may vary.

I want a companion to be friendly, but not too friendly; to be talkative, but not too talkative; to have a good dog, but not quite as good as mine; to have a sense of humor without being a humorist—and for God's sake, not a punster! I also want a companion who is a good shot, but not too damned good. The first rule of companionship in hunting is not to embarrass the other fellow.

Surely not the least of my pleasures in hunting and fishing is getting back home. And having somebody there who is glad I'm back and is interested in the kind of day I've had, someone to call out, "Any luck?"

"More luck than I'll probably ever know," I *could* answer. "My companion and I have been handling guns all day, I have driven 150 miles over dangerous highways, and I am still alive. If that isn't luck, I don't know what is. Just getting back home can be an achievement. Many people don't."

I could say that, but I don't. This is a time for relaxation, not morbid moralizing. So I'll say, "Yes, a wonderful day. There will never be another exactly like it."

"Any birds?"

"Yes, I brought back some and left some, and it is possible that those I left gave me as much pleasure as those I brought home. There is only one thing you can do with a dead bird, you know—eat it."

Upland game hunter in spectacular light. (Photograph © Bill Marchel)

BROWN BEAR THE HARD WAY

By Bob Brister

Bob Brister is an all-around sportsman, former guide, and shooting champion, and served for nearly forty years as the outdoors editor for the *Houston Chronicle*. Author of *Shotgunning: The Art and the Science*, he is currently a contributing editor to *Field & Stream*. Brister has received dozens of national writing and photography honors and awards, including a Pulitzer Prize nomination, the National Wildlife Federation's prestigious Special Achievement Award in Conservation, and the Outdoor Writers Association of America's top writing honor, the Excellence in Craft Award.

"Brown Bear the Hard Way," an unforgettable tale of a grizzly hunt that ultimately becomes a battle for survival, was first published in *Field & Stream*.

A Kodiak brown bear, the largest of the grizzlies. (Photograph © D. Robert Franz)

HAP MATHIS WAS breaking trail through a dense alder thicket when suddenly he dropped to one knee and flipped the sling of his .458 off his packboard in one swift, smooth motion. A few yards ahead was something big and dark in the brush. Instantly I had the two-power scope on it, and when I started laughing Hap looked around incrediously.

"It's no bear," I told him, "just a pile of dirt."

From our position, the mound looked almost exactly the size of a big, dark Alaska brown bear. But Hap still wasn't laughing.

"Start backing up the way we came," he whispered. "Get to that clearing over there, and be ready to shoot in a hurry if you have to!"

Backtracking uphill through dense alder bushes is not easy, and when we finally made the clearing I pantingly demanded to know what all the excitement was about.

"If there had been a bear working on that new den in there, he just might have showed you," the oldtimer grumbled. "You live around those big devils forty years like I have and you just may change some of your Texas ideas about bears. Two guides got killed not far from here a couple of years ago because they stumbled up on a bear working on his den. Both had rifles, too, and got off a shot. But at the range we walked in on that den, one shot ain't likely to stop a big bear in time."

He handed me his binoculars, and I could make out the dark hole in the side of the steep, alder-thick ravine. The dirt around it was fresh, with some huge tracks not yet covered by the light mixture of snow and rain which had been falling all morning.

"Brownies are strange bears some ways " Hap mumbled around his ever-present pipe. "Let's just sit here a minute and see what happens. My judgment tells me there's a bear right here close someplace, and he's probably seen us close to his den. If so, he ain't gonna like it; a bear knows he's helpless when he goes into hibernation, and he just doesn't like the idea of any two-legged critters knowing where his hideout is. You see the size of those tracks in that fresh dirt?"

For half an hour we sat there, watching the alders and the slope below which led down to a gurgling, snow-fed creek called "Hot Springs." We were near the base of whitecapped Mount Peulik on the Alaskan Peninsula some eighty miles from the little fishing town and U.S.

Air Force base at King Salmon. On the other side of the mountain, nearly twenty miles away and a hard day's walk up and down dozens of brushy ravines and hummocks in the tundra, was our base camp—outfitter Ray Loesche's snug, isolated cabins on the shore of Lake Ugashik.

As the falling rain began turning to snow, I wondered how wise we'd been to backpack into this remote valley. There was no place to land an airplane and we knew in advance we'd be confronted with a blizzard before we could walk back out again.

It had all started back in my home town, Houston, Texas, when one of my hunting partners, Houston architect Kenneth Campbell, invited Alaskan guide Ray Loesche and me to the same informal dinner at his home. Loesche was in Texas at the time booking hunts for the following year, and during the evening he mentioned a particularly big brown bear which he'd seen several times from the air in a little valley where no plane could land.

That sort of bear—and challenge—appealed to me. And in the comfort of Kenneth Campbell's living room I decided that backpacking in after an old monster that had been isolated for years would be a wonderful idea.

Now, shivering, wet to the skin, I pondered the radio reports we'd heard that morning of an incoming blizzard. In late October in that part of Alaska, we were asking for trouble.

Ray Loesche had not exactly liked the idea, but Hap Mathis, then his assistant guide, is an oldtimer in his 60's, a native of Alaska, and he helped me convince Loesche that it was a now-or-never situation; if the blizzard was very severe the bears would go into hibernation and the object of my hunt would be covered over in snow.

Since Campbell was after a giant moose he and Loesche had located, it was decided that Hap and I would go alone. We packed bedrolls, food, a small tent, and some emergency rations. Even if we got holed in for a few days, we could walk in around the base of the mountain. And when the weather let up we knew Loesche could fly over and drop in more supplies. With a little luck we could find that big boar of Hot Springs Valley and be on our way back before the bad weather ever hit. It all sounded so simple.

The walk in had taken almost all day because I'd

Stalking a grizzly is the greatest big-game challenge. (Photograph © Henry H. Holdsworth/Wild by Nature)

persisted in stalking some caribou for pictures, and when we finally made Hot Springs Creek we were both tired and the weather was already starting to change. We'd stashed our heavy gear, including the food and bedrolls, in a little ravine near the creek and had gone on upstream looking for bear sign before making camp.

That was a bad mistake, and I made another when I killed more time by demanding to take pictures of the bear's den. Hap finally relented but first made me fire a couple of shots in the air to make sure the bear wasn't in there. The two shots reverberated up and down the valley—and nothing happened.

So we walked carefully down to the den and I realized just how large an Alaskan brown bear's winter residence can be. From the tracks, this was obviously a big boar, and Hap showed me how he'd selected the exact spot in the steep bank of the ravine where snow would pile up heaviest. Thus, the entrance would be protected through the winter by several feet of snow.

With gun shouldered, I eased into the gloomy interior, stopped to let my eyes adjust, and realized that the den enlarged to a circular "room" somewhat larger than the entrance. The bear had been working on it that day, judging from the loose dirt that fell on me every time I bumped the ceiling. It was still damp where his giant claws had scraped out earth and roots. Hap was outside clamoring for us to get started, and when I came out of the den I carefully flipped on the rubber scope cover to keep out the snow and rain.

We walked straight down to the creek, forced our way through the dense alders, and found we'd picked a spot too wide to jump. Hap went one way to look for a crossing, and I went the other.

I'd gone maybe 25 yards when there was a sudden, deep-throated "Wuuuff" and a huge, dark mountain of fur rose up above the alders. He was so close I could see his hair rippling in the wind, and in that split second he dropped down out of sight again and I could hear alders crashing.

Instinctively I'd flipped the rifle sling upwards and off the packboard, and took a precious second to clear the scope—all the time thinking I'd muffed my chance at the biggest bear I'd ever seen.

Then suddenly an alder swayed and the next instant a dark shape was crashing through like a freight train heading straight for Hap. I filled the scope with brown hair and brush and shot, and with a roaring, snarling, ground-jarring crash the bear rolled and broke brush, biting at the wound. When he came up, as if in slow motion, I saw him turn and come for me, and the gun seemed to fire itself head on into the bulk of brown hair and exploding brush. He rolled like a monstrous ball into the opening beside the creek, snarling and biting at his shoulder, and in the same instant was up and coming again. The bolt worked, slammed shut, and I knew it would be the last time; I'd have to save the shot until I could put it between his eyes at pointblank range. With only the creek and 10 yards between us I could see nothing in the scope, could only point the gun as a shotgun, holding for his head. And as the gun bellowed the bear jumped the creek and I knew I'd hit low. But then he hesitated, shuddered, and slowly collapsed like a huge brown tent into the edge of the creek.

Hap came ripping through the alders, pipe smoking like a chimney, yelling and slapping me on the back. "By God, I never saw a bolt-action fired like a machinegun before;" he whooped, "and thank God

The ultimate game animal. (Photograph © D. Robert Franz)

for it . . . I couldn't shoot with the back of that fat Texas head in my sights the whole time!"

It was then, for the first time, I realized what had happened in that time lapse of seconds. The bear had apparently been in the thicket beside the creek, stalking us or perhaps just hiding and believing at the last moment we'd found him. At any rate he had charged Hap, giving me that first crossing shot, which apparently had been a good one. When he'd rolled and turned for me, I'd stepped to the right from behind an alder to shoot . . . and Hap said at that instant I almost lost the back of my head—he'd been already starting to squeeze off his .458 when I popped out in front of him.

We both sat down, shivering suddenly from the combination of excitement and cold, and it occurred to me that we were being rather confident. There was a giant bear lying less than ten steps away which hadn't yet been proven dead or alive. "Don't worry about that," Hap chuckled. "I saw the fur fly that last shot; you made a perfect neck shot, best there is on a bear that close; who taught you to do that?"

I told him I'd held between the eyes and missed when the bear jumped, and he shook his head. "At that angle," he said, "you'd better be glad you missed; a bear's skull is thick and the slug might have glanced off with his head down and coming; lucky or not, you got him in the right place."

We eased up to the bear and Hap poked his eye with the .458. But it was all over. Judging from his position and the entrance holes of the bullets, my first shot had taken him in the shoulder, the second had gone through his leg and then into the chest as he rolled and roared coming up for me, and the third broke his neck. Neither of the first two would have stopped him in time, Hap decided.

"Look at those worn-down teeth," he whistled. "Now he's an old one for sure! See those porcupine quills in his lips and tongue? There's reason enough right there for him to be in a bad humor. He must have been having a tough time getting food to take on a porcupine." I pulled open the huge jaws and saw that the bear had indeed been in pain; his teeth were worn down and rotting with cavities, and two big porcupine quills were imbedded in his tongue while several more quills stuck in his lips.

"But look at this if you want enough reason for him to be mad at two-legged critters," Hap was saying. On the side of his head the bear had a long, ugly bullet scar. The shot had creased his jaw, then plowed into the top of his back—just missing the backbone.

With a sudden chill I wondered whether that hunter is still alive. From the angle of the shot, the bear had to be coming head on. Had the shot turned him, or had this been the same giant bear that killed those two guides two years before? One of them had gotten off a shot.

"You better quit speculating about that other hunter and worry about us," Hap grumbled. "It'll be dark before we're done skinning him, and it ain't gonna be easy as you think to find our gear down there."

I offered to walk down the creek, find the equipment, and get a fire started so we'd have no trouble finding it. The snow was beginning to stick to the ground, and the thought occurred to me that it could cover our little spike camp in a matter of minutes. But Hap shook his head. "Your friend here will weigh close to 1,400 pounds," he said. "I can't turn him over to skin him by myself, and unless we get this hide off him right now, we'll never get it off. It's gonna be freezing on him as soon as his body heat leaves him."

Hap seemed maddeningly slow with the skinning and fleshing tools, but he reminded me that the more fat he could get off the hide the easier we could carry it out. "If I do a real good job," he puffed, "the hide will still weigh over a hundred pounds, maybe a hundred and a half."

When he finally rolled up the dark rug and lashed it to his packboard, I argued that I should carry it; Hap is twenty years my senior. But he grumbled that Texans know very little about Alaskan packboards, and puffing his pipe like a bandy-legged steam engine, he made the last moments of daylight count. It was pitch dark when we reached the bend in the creek near our spike camp, and Hap wasn't sure if it was upstream or down from us.

Rather than take a chance on getting separated in the dark, he kept the flashlight and stayed put to signal me back to him while I took off upstream looking for our tiny pile of equipment. I began falling through the ice of little swamps and stumbling into hummocks and holes in the tundra called "tules" until my legs began to get rubbery. Still no sign of the equipment. The falling snow had covered everything—it was a futile search.

When I gave up and turned to go back to Hap, I expected the wind to be at my back. It was the only reference point I had in the dark to maintain direction. Instead, it was blowing straight into my face. Was I lost that easily? Then I realized the wind had a different, icy bite to it. The blizzard had arrived, and instantly I knew Hap and I could be in serious trouble. We were both wet and the weather forecast had called for the temperature to drop down to zero.

Snow began blowing almost horizontally with the rising wind, and I had trouble making out even the outline of the brush. I was tiring fast from the repeated falls and trip-ups in the dark. I fired a signal shot and listened; if I could get the exact direction to him some precious steps could be saved. For nearly five minutes there was no answering shot, and a sort of numb panic gripped me. Why didn't he answer? Was the wind so strong he couldn't even hear the rifle? All I had was a metal match to start an emergency fire, a couple of candybars, and a soaked-through parka that was beginning to freeze stiff on my back.

Then I heard the heavy boom of the .458 straight ahead. I lunged through the brush, falling and getting up again, and finally saw the beam of Hap's flashlight probing up against the clouds like a miniature searchlight. The old trapper and woodsman had known I probably couldn't see the flashlight because of the brush and the ridges, but I could see that beam against the low clouds and sky.

When I reached him, utterly exhausted, Hap was shivering on his knees, trying to start a fire. The wood was wet, now frozen, but he had used a hatchet to cut some of the larger alder trunks and then split them open to get the wood in the very middle of each tree. He had his "fire insurance", a two-inch stub of a candle, lit and had made a pyramid of shavings and tiny sticks. But every time the fire would try to flame up the snow would put it out.

* * * *

Glassing for game from high mountain tundra, Alaska. (Photograph © Ron Spomer)

I took off my parka and made a windbreak of it, using my body to shield the wind and the parka to keep off the snow. The tiny blaze flickered and with numbed fingers we tried to whittle more dry sticks. For the first hour the fire was only a smoking, smouldering hope. But finally it was large enough to begin drying out the larger limbs. I looked at my watch and it was almost midnight. We had seven more hours until there would be daylight enough to find our sleeping bags and food.

The exertion of walking after and chopping wood began to take more and more effort; the temptation was just to lie down and go to sleep. Twice the hatchet slipped out of my numbed fingers and once it glanced off the knee of my hip boot. How stupid can fingers be just because they are cold? I found myself talking out loud to them.

Our clothes had begun freezing on our backs, and we dragged the bear hide to the fire, thawed the leather thongs binding it to the packboard, and rolled it out on the ground, hair side up. Then we wrapped ourselves up in it together to utilize our combined body heat and the thick hide's insulation to break the cold.

I had begun shivering uncontrollably, which Hap said was because of the exhaustion of nearly three hours of stumbling in the snow and tundra hunting for our gear. He told me to try and sleep, and finally in the protection of the hide some of the shivering began to subside. I woke up sometime later, checked to see if the fire was still alive, and tried to get up to put more wood on it. I couldn't move at all!

Hap awoke with my movements and helped me rock the hide back and forth; we were mummies in a frozen bearhide for a moment or so, but then the hide cracked loose and we pried it apart. The rest of the night we took turns chopping alder limbs, devoting half of them to the fire and the other half to building up a lean-to shelter for snow to bank against.

The wind kept howling higher, scattering our fire, so we began lying beside it on our sides to shield the fire and to warm one side while the other froze. Twice I got too close and the collar of my down jacket caught fire and burned my neck. I didn't realize it until I smelled it.

When daybreak finally came, 2 feet of snow covered the ground and the odds of finding our food and equipment had gone down with the temperature. Nothing looked the same, and we were so tired there could be no staggering around with a 150-pound bear hide.

"We've got to find some kind of shelter," Hap decided. "We can't travel until this blizzard quits."

Then I thought of the bear's den. It was close, and it would be warm and big enough for both of us. Also, the carcass of the bear was close and it would certainly be enough to feed us. We left the hide by the remains of the fire and marked it by hanging my blaze-orange hiking pack atop a close-by alder bush. Then we walked across the ridge and found the den.

We were so cold we just walked in—probably too fast—but there was no bear, and for the first time we were protected from the wind. Instantly we started warming up and feeling better. Hap cut some wood and we made a fire at the entrance, then found there was enough of a chimney effect at the entrance that we could bring the fire inside. We moved several burning sticks in, and for the first time in hours got thoroughly, smokily warm.

Hap thawed the tough, red meat we'd hacked from the frozen carcass and we roasted it until it was burned on the outside. He said most bears have trichinosis, and the heat kills the germs. With or without germs, it was delicious; twenty-four hours had passed since we had eaten anything but a candybar each.

By midafternoon it was obvious the blizzard would be a two- or three-day affair and we'd have to spend another night. Shortly before dawn the wind changed, and we knew it immediately, because suddenly the den was full of smoke.

"We're rested and full of grub as we're ever gonna be," Hap decided. "Let's just go get that bear hide and start for base camp; longer we wait the deeper the snow's gonna be."

I asked about our sleeping bags.

"Hell with them," he grinned. "We'll mail yours to you next spring. We got all the load we can carry in this snow and the shape we're in now."

As soon as it was light we started out, and I was glad there were only a couple of feet of snow. Everything was covered over and it was like walking in the dark again; we couldn't see the holes in the tundra. I was also glad there were two of us; when one fell down the other could pull forward on his packboard to get him up again. Without help, I don't think either one of us could have made it.

Finally we cleared a ridge and could see the blue expanse of Lake Ugashik below. Our base camp cabins were tiny, dark dots against the snow. They looked close, but there were half a dozen creeks and ravines with steep, brushy sides to be crossed and we were getting very tired. Again I had that strange sensation of just wanting to lie down in the snow and go to sleep. We stopped to eat our last candybar and Hap developed leg cramps when he tried to get up with the bear hide. I switched packs with him and realized what a terrific load this man 60 years old had been carrying all along. He had to be tough!

The last few hours are not clear; just an interminable expanse of snow, stopping to breathe on the ridges, wanting to lie down and sleep. Hap was worrying we couldn't make the cabins by dark, but I was too tired and cold to worry. We just kept walking.

Kenneth Campbell had been outside in the yard of the cabin making some pictures of the trophy moose rack he'd killed and happened to see us coming across the willow flats. Thinking we'd had our sleeping bags and food along, he started yelling and joking at us from a distance . . . and then he saw the looks of us.

Only a few yards away were those wonderful warm cabins, hot coffee, whiskey, and food. It was all over . . . that long, cold, hard night of the bear.

A bearskin broad enough to warm half a dozen hunters. (Photograph courtesy the California Historical Society)

ABOVE: *Fully loaded hunters on an Alaskan ridge. (Photograph © Ron Spomer)*

LEFT: *A grizzly looks eerily human wading through a glacial river. (Photograph © Jeff Foott)*

SHARE AND SHARE ALIKE

By Patrick F. McManus

Patrick McManus has a gift for elevating the relatively mundane—in this case dividing up big-game animals between hunters—to a level of hilarity rarely, if ever, attained by other outdoors writers. The man is just plain funny, a quality that has stood him well in writing his wildly enjoyable columns for *Outdoor Life,* where he has served as editor-at-large since 1981. McManus's stories have been collected into several books, including *A Fine and Pleasant Misery* (1978), *They Shoot Canoes, Don't They?* (1981), *The Grasshopper Trap* (1985), *The Night the Bear Ate Goombaw* (1989), and *The Good Samaritan Strikes Again* (1992).

"Share and Share Alike" first appeared in the October 1982 issue of *Outdoor Life,* and was later included in *Never Sniff a Gift Fish* (1983).

This hunter is quickly getting over the thrill of getting his game and is contemplating the daunting task of butchering his moose. Dividing it up among the hunting party will be the next daunting problem. (Photograph © Ron Spomer)

THE SHARING OF a single big-game animal between two hunters is at once the most delicate and the most complex problem encountered in hunting, with the possible exception of deciding whose vehicle to drive on the hunt. It may be useful to examine the problem in some detail.

Let us begin with a hypothetical situation. As is well known, an elk that is shot dead within fifteen feet of your hunting vehicle will still pull himself together enough to gallop to the very bottom of the steepest canyon within five miles. This is known as the elk's revenge. Assume you have just shot such an elk. You and your hunting partner, whom we'll call Bob, have tracked the elk to the bottom of the canyon. As you stand over the massive form of the felled but still magnificent animal, you become contemplative. One of the things you contemplate is how much bigger an elk is at the bottom of a canyon than it is fifteen feet from your vehicle. (Scientists have calculated that a wounded elk will add fifty pounds to its weight for every hundred yards it gallops down into a canyon.) You now ask yourself two questions: (1) How are you going to lug the elk back up to your vehicle? and (2) Why didn't you go golfing today instead of hunting?

With three round trips each, you and Bob manage to pack out the elk section by section. Neither of you experiences any extraordinary ill effects from the exertion, other than the seizing up of major portions of your cardiovascular systems. Bob lies wheezing by the side of the road, a haunch of elk still strapped to his back. You are walking around on your knees and mumbling about "getting in shape" and not caring if you "never see another *bleeping* elk." At this point you are willing to give the entire elk to Bob, provided that he lives. Your intimate association with elk meat over the preceding hours has diminished your appetite for the stuff and has resulted in a psychological malfunction known as excessive generosity. Wisely, you put off the decision of what share of the elk should go to Bob until you are rested and your mind has cleared.

The culinary aspects of elk meat improve in direct proportion to distance in time from the packing-out process. A week after the hunt, during which time the elk has been aging nicely in a cooler, the thought of all those steaks and roasts stashed away for the winter is intensely satisfying. There is still the problem of what

portion of the elk should be Bob's share. You are now in the proper frame of mind to make this decision.

Your reasoning goes something like this: For openers, you consider giving Bob half the elk. Once you have enjoyed a few moments of mirth over this ridiculous notion, you get down to serious figuring. Using half an elk as base, you deduct from it five pounds for each day remaining in the elk season, days in which Bob might very well shoot his own elk. You make further deductions for the amount of whining Bob did while packing out your elk. Then there is the matter of that unseemly phrase Bob blurted out when he learned the elk you had shot was at the bottom of a three-thousand-foot canyon—more deductions, all of them choice cuts. You don't forget Bob's tripping over a log and cartwheeling down the slope with a hindquarter strapped to his packboard. That bruised a lot of meat, some of which was elk. Further deductions. When you finally total the figures, you discover that Bob now owes you approximately one quarter of an elk. The charlatan hasn't even had the courtesy to mention the matter of this debt to you. And to think you trusted him enough to let him help pack your elk out of a three-thousand-foot canyon! Some gratitude!

In the end, your calculations are for naught. Your spouse demands that you give Bob a generous share of the elk. You acquiesce reluctantly but eventually conclude she was right—although this conclusion does not arrive until the middle of April, when even the thought of one more elk roast blights your day.

"What's for supper?" you ask your wife.

"Elk," she replies.

"*Aaaack!*" you say. "How about TV dinners? I'm sick of elk!"

"You shot it, you eat it."

"I know, I'll call Bob. He would probably like some more elk."

"Are you kidding?" Bob responds. "I'm fed up to my follicles with elk! I couldn't choke down another bite of elk if I lived to be five hundred!"

"Oh yes you can and you are! You didn't take your full share of the elk! You packed it out and you're going to eat it!"

In this way, the problem of sharing a single big-game animal between hunters usually resolves itself.

My first encounter with the problem of sharing a

A Montana deer hunter returns with his kill. (Photograph © Alan and Sandy Carey)

big-game animal occurred when I was sixteen. I was hunting with my cousin, Buck, who was several years older than I. At that time, Buck was at the height of his intellectual powers and knew all there was to know about hunting and most of everything else. Some people are stingy with their knowledge and try to hoard it, but not Buck. He handed his out freely and voluminously and endlessly, at all hours of the day or night, whether one was in the market for knowledge or not. Naturally, because of his towering intellect and absolute knowledge of all matters pertaining to hunting, Buck got to devise our field tactics.

Shortly after dawn, as Buck was bathing my semi-consciousness with a steady stream of his hunting knowledge, I glanced up the side of the mountain to clear the glaze from my eyes and spotted five specks. The specks were moving.

"Buck, there's a herd of mule deer up there!" I shouted.

Since part of Buck's knowledge consisted of the natural law that he was the only one who could spot deer first, he dismissed my report with a chuckle and the comment that the specks I saw were probably on my glasses.

Then he stopped the car and got out, casually, as if to stretch and satisfy a need for a breath of fresh air. He got back in the car, shook a cigarette from a pack, lit it, blew out the match. "There's a herd of mule deer about halfway up the mountain," he said. "When you're driving out to hunt mule deer, it's a good idea to stop every once in a while and check the slopes. Now you take these deer here, we might have missed them if I hadn't stopped for a look around."

"Good, Buck, good. I'll try to remember that."

Buck then laid out the tactics. "Now here's what we're going to do. You work your way up the mountain toward the deer. I'll drive around to the top of the mountain and wait on the road just in case they try to cut back over the ridge."

"Why don't you climb the mountain and I drive around on the road?"

"Because it wouldn't work, that's why. Besides, if the deer cut back over the ridge, we want to have the best shot to be waiting there."

"Oh."

I got out to start working my way up the mountain, and Buck drove off, leisurely smoking his cigarette and fiddling with the radio dials. There was about a foot of new snow on the mountain, and the climb was cold, slippery, and exhausting. Occasionally a fir tree would unload a bough of snow down the back of my neck, and that didn't improve my mood, either. Nor did the thought of Buck sitting in the warm car at the top of the mountain, drinking hot coffee from the thermos and smoking and listening to the radio, while he gave the deer time to detect my presence and then retreat practically into his lap.

But it didn't work out that way. All at once I found myself right in the middle of the herd of mule deer. A nice little buck stepped from behind a tree and stared at me, as if astonished to find a human being stupid enough to be climbing a snow-covered mountain that early in the morning. I downed him with a single shot. The rest of the herd raced off in all directions, except toward Buck. An hour later I was back down on the road with my deer. Buck, who had witnessed the "whole fiasco," as he called it, was waiting for me. He was hot, too.

"Boy, that was dumb!" he snarled. "Shooting that itty-bitty buck when there was one three times as big

Three hunters and their portly jackrabbit return home to divide the spoils. (Photograph courtesy Roger Welsch)

An elk wades in a foggy Wyoming lake. (Photograph © Thomas D. Mangelsen/Images of Nature)

in the herd. I knew I shouldn't give you the best chance, but since you're just a kid and all, I thought I'd do you the favor. Boy, did you blow it!"

We rode in silence all the way home, Buck occupied with what I could easily guess were dire thoughts, and I, with gloating. When you're sixteen and wear glasses and aren't that good at sports and spend a good deal of time in the company of an intellectual giant, you don't get much opportunity for gloating. When you do, you savor it.

"You just remember," Buck said, after dropping me and my deer off home, "part of that deer is mine."

When I got around to cutting up the deer, I at first considered giving Buck a full half of it. On the other hand, I had my mother, grandmother, and sister to pro-

vide wild game for, and Buck lived by himself in an apartment. If he tried to eat half a deer all by himself, he would soon become sick of venison and wouldn't want to go deer hunting ever again. No, I told myself, it would be better if I gave him only a hindquarter. That would be about right for one person.

On the other hand, steaks cut from the hindquarter of a deer are awfully good eating. Buck might use a venison-steak dinner as bait to lure one of his girl friends into his apartment. That in all probability could lead to Buck and the girl committing a serious sin. Since my religion forbade even contributing to serious sin, I was not about to risk going to hell over a hindquarter of venison. No sir, Buck would have to make do with a front quarter.

ABOVE: *Comradely hunters with freshly killed game—but the relations among the hunters likely became much more testy when it was time to divide the bear six ways. (Photograph used by permission, Utah State Historical Society, all rights reserved)*

FACING PAGE: *A bugling Rocky Mountain elk. (Photograph © Mark and Jennifer Miller Photos)*

But which front quarter? That presented no real difficulty. Because of Buck's interest in science, he would be intrigued by studying the effect of a .30/30 slug on the shoulder of a deer. There was still a lot of good meat on the shoulder, too.

Upon further consideration, I decided that Buck might prefer to forgo his scientific studies and have the shoulder ground up into venison burger. So I ground up the venison for him.

Well, that turned out to be an awful lot of venison burger for one person. I started dividing it up into neat little piles, until I found the exact amount that I thought would be suitable for Buck. I then left his share on the table while I went to deposit the rest of the venison in the cold storage locker.

A few days later I ran into Buck. "Hey, you little rat," he greeted me, "where's my share of our deer?"

I shook my head sadly. "You may have some trouble believing this, Buck, but while I was taking my share down to the locker, the cat got in the house and ate your share."

Buck did not take the news well.

THE UNCLOUDED DAY

By E. Annie Proulx

E. Annie Proulx is not well known as a hunting writer. Then again, she's not well known as a cooking author, though she is the author of *The Complete Dairy Foods Cookbook: How To Make Everything from Cheese to Custard in Your Own Kitchen* (1982). She isn't often asked for advice on landscaping, but she is indeed the author of *Plan and Make Your Own Fences and Gates, Walkways, Walls and Drives* (1983). Throughout her twenty-five-year freelance career, she has proven able to tackle a wide range of subjects—including the pursuit of game.

Of course, she *is* well known as one of the great fiction writers of the late twentieth century, having received the PEN/Faulkner Award for Fiction for her book *Postcards* (1992) and the National Book Award for Fiction and the Pulitzer Prize, among several other honors, for her wonderful and hilarious book *The Shipping News* (1993).

This fictional grouse-hunting piece first appeared in the anthology *Seasons of the Hunter,* a first-class collection of original stories edited by Robert Elman and David Seybold.

Grouse hunters and setters afield. (Photograph © Ron Spomer)

IT WAS A rare thing, a dry, warm spring that swelled into summer so ripe and full that gleaming seed bent the grass low a month before its time; a good year for grouse. When the season opened halfway through September, the heat of summer still held, dust lay like yellow flour on the roads, and a perfume of decay came from the thorned mazes where blackberries fell and rotted on the ground. Grouse were in the briars, along the watercourses, and, drunk on fermenting autumn juices, they flew recklessly, their wings cleaving the shimmering heat of the day.

Santee did not care to hunt birds in such high-colored weather. Salty sweat stung the whipped-branch welts on his neck and arms, the dog worked badly, and the birds spoiled in an hour. In their sour, hot intestines he smelled imminent putrefaction. The feathers stuck to his hands, for Earl would not gut them. Noah, the dog, lay panting in the pulsating shade.

The heat wave wouldn't break. Santee longed for the cold weather and unclouded days that lay somewhere ahead, for the sharp chill of spruce shadow, icy rime thickening osier twigs, and a hard autumnal sky cut by the parabolic flights of birds in the same way pond ice was cut by skaters. Ah goddamn, thought Santee, there were better things to do than hunt partridge with a fool in these burning days.

Earl had come to Santee the year before and begged him to teach him how to hunt birds. He had a good gun, he said, a Tobias Hume. Santee thought it overrated and overpriced, but it was a finer instrument than his field-grade Jorken with the cracked stock he'd meant to replace for years. (The rough walnut blank lay on the workbench out in the barn, cans of motor oil and paint standing on it, and the kids had ruined the checkering files by picking out butternut meats with them.) Santee's gun, like its owner, was inelegant and long in the tooth, but it worked well.

Earl had come driving up through the woods to Santee's place, overlooking the mess in the yard, nodding to Verna, and he had flattered Santee right out of his mind.

"Santee," he said, measuring him, seeing in which certain ways he was inclined, "I've talked to people around and they say you're very good. I want to learn how to hunt birds. I want you to teach me. I'll pay you to teach me everything about them."

Santee could see that Earl had money. He wore nice boots, rich corduroy trousers in a golden syrup color, his hands were as well shaped as doves, and his voice rolled out of his throat like sweet batter. He was not more than thirty, Santee thought, looking at the firm cheek stabs and thick yellow hair.

"I usually hunt by myself," Santee said, giving each word its fair measure of weight. "Me'n the dog." Noah, lying on the porch under the rusty glider, raised his head at the sound of the words "hunt" and "birds" and "dog" and watched them.

"Nice dog," said Earl in his confectionery voice. Santee folded his arms across his chest rather than let them hang by his sides. Hands in the pockets was even worse, a wastrel's posture. Earl's hands were in his pockets.

Earl oiled Santee with his voice. "All I ask, Santee, is that you try it two or three times, and if you don't want to continue, why then . . . I'll pay for your time." He gave Santee a smile, the leaf-colored eyes under the gleaming, swollen lids shifting from Santee to the warped screen door, to the scabby paint on the clapboards, to the run-down yard. Santee looked off to the side as though the muscles in his own eyes were weak, and said, "Maybe give it a try. Rather go out on a weekday than a weekend. You get away on Monday?" Earl could get away any day Santee wanted. He worked at home.

"What doin'?" asked Santee, letting his arms hang down.

"Consulting. I analyze stock and economic trends." Santee saw that Earl was younger than his own oldest son, Derwin, whose teeth were entirely gone and who worked up at the veneer mill in Potumsic Falls breathing fumes and tending a machine with whirling, curved blades. Santee said he would go out with Earl on Monday. He didn't know how to say no.

The first morning was a good one, a solid bright day with a spicy taste to the air. Noah was on his mettle, eager to find birds and showing off a little for the stranger. Santee set Earl some distance away on his right until he could see how he shot.

Noah worked close. He stiffened two yards away from birds in front, he pointed birds to the left, the right. A step from Santee or Earl sent partridge bursting out of the cover and into straightaway flight. He

A hunter holds his side-by-side shotgun. (Photograph © Bill Buckley/The Green Agency)

pinned them in trees and bushes, scented them feeding on fallen fruit or dusting in powdery bowls of fine earth, marked them as they pattered through wood sorrel. He worked like two dogs, his white sides gliding through the grass, his points so rigid he might have been a glass animal, and the grouse tore up the air, the shotguns bellowed. Earl, Santee saw, didn't know enough to say "Nice dog" when it counted.

Santee held himself back in order to let his pupil learn, but Earl was a very slow, poor shot. The bird would be fifty yards out and darting through safe holes in the air when Earl finally got the gun around and pulled the trigger. Sometimes a nervous second bird

would go up before Earl fired at the first one. He couldn't seem to catch the rhythm, and had excuses for each miss.

"Caught the butt end in my shirt-pocket flap," he'd say, laughing a little, and "My fingers are stiff from carrying the gun," and "Oh, that one was gone before I could get the bead on him."

Santee tried over and over again to show him that you didn't aim at the bird, that you just . . . threw up the gun and fired in the right place.

"You have to shoot where they're goin', not where they are." He made Earl watch him on the next one, how the gun notched into place on his shoulder, how

1985 ~ The Unclouded Day / 177

his right elbow lifted smoothly as his eyes bent toward the empty air the bird would enter in a second. *Done!* went the shotgun, and the bird fell like a nut.

"Now you do it," said Santee.

But when a grouse blustered out of the wild rose haws, Earl only got the gun to his hip, then twisted his body in an odd backward contortion as he fired. The train of shot cut a hole in the side of a tamarack and the bird melted away through the trees.

"I'n see you need a lot of practice," said Santee.

"What I need *is* practice," agreed Earl, "and that is what I am paying for."

"Try movin' the stock up to your shoulder," said Santee, thinking his kids had shot better when they were eight years old.

They worked through the morning, Santee illustrating swift reaction and tidy speed, and Earl sweating and jerking like an old Vitagraph film, trying to line up the shotgun with the bird. Santee shot seven grouse and gave four to Earl, who had missed every one. Earl gave Santee a hundred dollars and said he wanted to do it again.

"I can practice all the rest of this week," he said, making it sound like a piano lesson.

The next three Mondays were the same. They went out and worked birds. Earl kept shooting from the hip. With his legs spraddled out he looked like an old-time gangster spraying the rival mob with lead.

"Listen here," said Santee, "there are six more weeks left in the season, which means we go out six more times. Now, I am not after more money, but you might want to think about goin' out a little more often." Earl was eager and said he'd pay.

"Three times a week. I can go Monday, Wednesday, and Friday." They tried it that way. Then they tried Monday, Tuesday, and Wednesday for the continuity. Earl was paying Santee three hundred dollars a week and he hadn't shot a single bird.

"How's about this?" said Santee, feeling more and more like a cheating old whore every time they went out. "How's about I come over to your place on the weekend with a box of clay pigeons and you practice shootin' them up? No charge! just to sort of get your eye in, and the gun up on your shoulder."

"Yes, but I'm not upset about missing the birds, you know," said Earl, looking in the trees. "I've read the books and I know it takes years before you develop that fluid, almost instinctive response to the grouse's rising thunder. I know, believe me, how difficult a target those elusive fast fliers really are, and I'm willing to work on it, even if it takes years."

Santee had not heard shooting birds was that hard, but he knew Earl was no good; he had the reflexes of a snowman. He said to Verna, "That Earl has got to get it together or I can't keep takin' his money. I feel like I'm goin' to the salt mines every time we go out. I don't have the heart to hunt anymore on my own, out of fear I'll bust up a bunch of birds he needs for practice. Dammit, all the fun is goin' out of it."

"The money is good," said Verna, giving the porch floor a shove that set the glider squeaking. Her apron was folded across her lap, her arms folded elbow over elbow with her hands on her shoulders, her ankles crossed against the coolness of the night. She wore the blue acrylic fur slippers Santee had given her for Mother's Day.

"I just wonder how I got into it," he said, closing his eyes and gliding.

He bought a box of a hundred clay pigeons and drove up to Earl's house on a Sunday afternoon. It was the kind of day people went for a ride.

"I wish I hadn't come now," said Verna, looking through the cloudy windshield at Earl's house, an enormous Swiss chalet with windows like tan bubbles in the roof and molded polystyrene pillars holding up a portico roof. She wouldn't get out of the truck, but sat for two hours with the window ground up. Santee knew how she felt, but he had to go. He was hired to teach Earl how to hunt birds.

There was a big porch, and on it was Earl's wife, as thin as a folded dollar bill, her hand as narrow and cold as a trout. A baby crawled around inside a green plastic-mesh pen playing with a tomato. Earl told them to watch.

"Watch Daddy shoot the birdy!" he said.

"Beady!" said the baby.

"Knock those beadies dead, Earl," said the wife in a sarcastic voice, drawing her fingernail through a drop

Grouse hunting on snowshoes. (Photograph © Tom Walker)

ABOVE: *An English setter on point in a autumnal bramble. (Photograph © Doug Stamm/ProPhoto)*

FACING PAGE: *The quarry: ruffed grouse. (Photograph © Robert E. Barber)*

of moisture from her drink, fallen on the chair arm, until it resembled a trailing comet, a streaking tear, a rivulet of rain on the windshield.

Santee cocked his arm back again and again and sent the pigeons flying out over a garden of dark shrubs. His ears rang. The baby screamed every time the gun went off, but Earl wouldn't let the woman take him inside.

"Watch!" he cried. "Dammit, watch Daddy shoot the beady!" He would get the gun to his hip and bend his back into the strange posture he had made his trademark. Him and Al Capone, thought Santee, saying "Put it to your shoulder" like a broken record. "It won't backfire."

He looked to see if Earl shut his eyes behind the yellow spectacles when he pulled the trigger, but couldn't tell. After a long time a clay round flew into three black pieces and Earl shrieked "I got it!" as if it were a woolly mammoth. It was the first object he had hit since Santee had met him.

"Pretty good," he lied, "*now* you're doin' it."

Verna called all the kids home for dinner a week later. There was home-cured ham basted with Santee's hard cider, baked Hubbard squash, mashed potato with thick Jersey cream spattered over each mound, and a platter of roast partridge glazed with chokecherry jelly. Before they sat down at the table Verna got them to clean up the yard. Derwin had borrowed the dump truck from the veneer mill. They all counted one-two-three and heaved the carcass of Santee's 1952 Chevrolet in with the torn chicken wire, rotted fence posts, and dimpled oil cans. Derwin drove the load to the dump after dinner and brought back a new lawn mower Verna had told him to get.

Another day she spent the morning wading the brook, feeling for spherical stones of a certain size with

A Chance to Double *(1994) by Bob
White. (Courtesy of the artist)*

her feet. Santee carried them up to the house in a grain bag. When they had dried on the porch she painted them snow white and set them in a line along the driveway. Santee saw the beauty of it—the green shorn grass, the gleaming white stones. It all had something to do with teaching Earl how to hunt birds, but aside from the money he didn't know what.

After a while he did know what. It was that she wouldn't let him quit. She would go out into the yard at the earliest light of hunting days—Santee had come to think of them as working days—walking in the wet grass and squinting at the sky to interpret the character of the new day. She got back in bed and put her cold feet on Santee's calves.

"It's cloudy," she would say. "Rain by noon." Santee would groan, because Earl did not like to get his gun wet.

"Won't it hurt it?" he always asked, as though he knew it would.

"Don't be no summer soldier," said Santee. "Wipe it down when you get back home and put some WD-40 to it, all good as new." It took him a while to understand that it wasn't the gun. Earl didn't like to get rain down his neck or onto his shooting glasses with the yellow lenses, didn't care to feel the cold drops trace narrow trails down his back and forearms, or to taste the salty stuff that trickled from his hatband to the corners of his mouth.

They were walking through deep wet grass, the rain drumming hard enough to make the curved blades bounce up and down. Earl's wet twill pants were plastered to him like blistered skin. Something in the way he pulled at the sodden cloth with an arched finger and thumb told Santee the man was angry at the rain, at him, maybe mad enough to quit giving Santee three hundred dollars a week for no birds and a wet nature walk. Good, thought Santee.

But the rain stopped and a watery sun warmed

BELOW: *A pair of upland hunters in a tallgrass field. (Photograph © Bill Buckley / The Green Agency)*

FACING PAGE: *The end of day afield for a hunter and his pup. (Photograph © Bill Buckley / The Green Agency)*

their backs. Noah found tendrils of rich hot grouse scent lying on the moist air as solidly as cucumber vines on the garden earth. He locked into his catatonic point again and again, and they sent the birds flying in arcs of shaken raindrops. Earl didn't connect, but he said he knew it took years before shooters got the hang of it.

The only thing he shot that season was the clay

Autumn grouse. (Photograph © Doug Stamm/ProPhoto)

pigeon, and the year ended with no birds for Earl, money in Santee's bank account, and a row of white stones under the drifting snow. Santee thought it was all over, a bad year to be buried in the memory with other bad years.

He never thought of Earl through the next spring and summer without a shudder. The droughty grouse

summer held into September. Santee bored the replacement stock for the Jorken. He bought a new checkering file and sat on the porch after dinner making a good job of it and waiting for the heat to break, thinking about going out by himself in the chill October days as the woods and fields faded to neutral grays and browns and the clods of earth froze hard. He hunched to the west on the steps, catching the last of the good light; the days were getting shorter, in spite of the lingering heat from the baked earth. Verna fanned her damp neck with a sale flier that had come in the mail.

"Car's comin'," she said. Santee stopped rasping and listened.

"It's that Earl again," said Verna.

He was a little slicker in his talk, and wore an expensive game vest with a rubber pocket in the back where the birds would lie, their dark blood seeping into the seams.

"My wife gave me this," he said, and he showed them the new leather case for his shotgun, stamped with his initials and a design of three flying grouse.

"No," Santee tried to say, "I've taught you all I can. I don't want to take your money anymore." But Earl wasn't going to let him go. He wanted something more than a teacher this time. He wanted a companion with a dog, and Santee was it, with no pay.

"After all, we got to know each other very well last year. We're a good team—friends," Earl said, looking at the fresh paint on the clapboards, "Nice job," he said.

Santee went because he was guilty. He had taken Earl's money the last season, and until the fool shot a bird on his own or gave up, Santee was obliged to keep going out with him. The thought that Earl might ruin every fall for the rest of his life made Santee sick.

"I've come to hate partridge huntin'," he told Verna in the sultry night. "I hate those white stones too." She knew what he was talking about.

Derwin heard Earl bragging down at the store, some clam dip and a box of Triscuits on the counter near his hand. Earl's new game vest hung open casually, his yellow shooting glasses hung outside the breast pocket, one earpiece tucked in through the buttonhole.

"Yes," he said, "we did quite well today. Limited out. I hunt with Santee, you know—grand old fellow."

"He didn't know who I was," raged Derwin, who had wanted to say something deadly but hadn't found any words until he drove up home and sat on the edge of the porch. "Whyn't you tell him where to head in, Daddy? At least quit givin' him birds he makes like he shot himself."

"I wish I could," groaned Santee. "If he would just get one bird I could cut loose, or if he decided to go in for somethin' else and quit comin' around. But I feel like I owe him part of a bargain. I took a lot of his money and all he got out of it was a clay pigeon."

"You don't owe him nothin'," said Derwin, but without conviction.

Earl came up again the next morning. He parked his Saab in the shade and beeped the horn in Santee's truck until he came out on the porch.

"Where you want to hit today?" called Earl. It wasn't a question. "Might as well take your truck, it's already scratched up." In some way he had gotten an advantage and Santee just followed along.

"I thought we'd go to the Africa covert and then hit White Birch Heaven." Earl had given fanciful names to the different places they hunted. "Africa" because there was long yellow grass on the edge of a field Earl said looked like the veldt. "White Birch Heaven" because Noah had pointed six birds in twenty minutes. Santee had taken two, leaving the rest for seed after Earl shot the tops out of the birches. They were gray birches, but Santee had not cared enough to say so, any more than he pointed out that the place had been called "Ayer's high pasture" for generations.

It was breathlessly close as they climbed toward the upper fields of the old farm. The sky was a slick, pearly-white color heated bubbling hot by the hidden sun. Noah lagged,

the dust filling his hot nose. Santee's shirt was wet with a sweat patch in the shape of Uganda, and he could feel thunder in the ground, the storm that had been building for weeks of drumming heat and endless cicada whine that went on and on, but was now failing and falling away like rain moving on to another part of the country. Deerflies and gnats bit furiously at their ears and necks. The leaves hung limp and yellowed, the soil crumbled under their feet.

"Gonna be a hell of a storm," said Santee.

Nothing moved. They might have been in a painted field, walking slowly across the fixed landscape where no bird could ever fly, nor tree fall.

"You won't put no birds up in this weather," said Santee.

Grouse silhouetted against the setting sun. (Photograph © Bill Marchel)

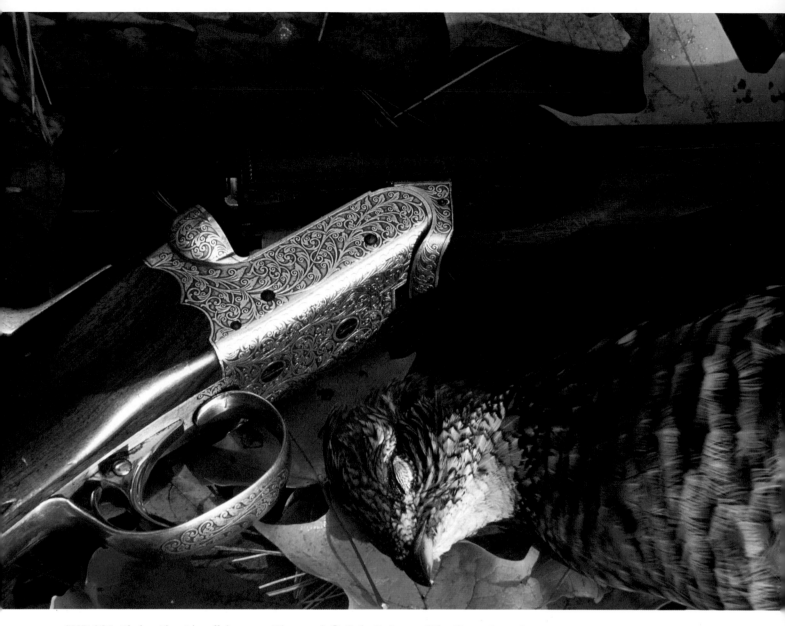

SKB 385 side-by-side with ruffed grouse. (Photograph © Dale C. Spartas/The Green Agency)

"What?" asked Earl, the yellow glasses shining on his turned face like insect eyes.

"I said it's gonna be a corker of a storm. See there?" Santee dropped his arm toward the west, where a dark humped line illuminated by veins of lightning lay across the horizon. "Comin' right for us like a house on fire. Time to go home and try another day."

He started back down, paying no attention to Earl's remarks that the storm was a long way off and there were birds up there. He was dogged enough, thought Santee sourly.

As they went down the hill, slipping on the drought-polished grass, the light thickened to a dirty ocher. Little puffs of wind raised dust and started the poplars vibrating.

"You might be right," said Earl, passing Santee. "It's coming along pretty fast. I just felt a drop." Santee looked back over his shoulder and saw the black wall of veined cloud had swollen high into the sky. Bursts of wind came ripping across the slope, and the rolling grind of thunder shook the earth. Noah scampered fearfully, his tail clamped between his legs, his eyes seeking Santee's again and again.

"We're goin', boy," said Santee encouragingly.

The first raindrops hit like bird shot, rattling down on them and striking the trees with flat smacks. White hail pellets bounced and stung where they hit flesh. They came into a belt of spruce at a half-run. There was a narrow opening in the trees like a bowling alley, and halfway down its length a panicky grouse flew straight away from them. It was at least eighty yards out, an impossible distance, when Earl heaved his shotgun onto his hip and fired. At the moment he pulled the trigger, lightning struck a spruce behind them. The grouse dropped low and skimmed away, but Earl believed he had hit it. He had not even heard the lightning strike, buried in the sound of his crashing gun.

"Get it!" he shouted at Noah, who had pasted himself to Santee's legs when the lightning cracked the tree. "Make your dog get it!" yelled Earl, pointing in the direction the grouse had flown. The rain roared down on them. Earl ran for a spruce shelter in the direction his bird had vanished, still pointing through the bursting rain. "Fetch! Fetch! Oh, you damn thing, fetch my bird!"

Santee, trusting the principle that lightning never strikes twice in the same place, sheltered under the smoking spruce. The bolt had entered the pith and exploded the heartwood in a column of live steam. White wood welled out of the riven bark. Almost at his feet, lying where they had fallen from the needled canopy of the top branches, were three dead grouse. They steamed gently in the cold rain. The hard drops struck the breast feathers like irregular heartbeats. Santee picked them up and looked at them. He turned them around and upside down. As soon as the rain slackened he pulled his shirt up over his head and made a run for Earl's tree.

"You don't need to yell at my dog. Here's your birds. Three in one shot, mister man, is somethin' I never seen before. You have sure learned how to shoot." He shook his head.

Earl's eyes were hidden behind the rain-streaked yellow shooting glasses. His thick cheeks were wet and his lips flapped silently, then he gabbled, "Something felt right," seizing the birds in his hands. "I knew something was going to happen today. I guess I was finally ready for the breakthrough."

He talked all the way back to Santee's truck, and as they drove up through the woods, the windshield wipers beating, the damp air in the cab redolent of wet dog, explained how he'd felt the birds were there, how he'd felt the gun fall into line on them, how he saw the feathers fountain up.

"I saw right where they went down," he said. Santee thought he probably believed he had. "But that dog of yours wouldn't retrieve. He's not my idea of an impartial dog."

Santee pulled up in his yard beside Earl's Saab and set the hand brake. The rain flowed over the windshield in sheets. Santee cleared his throat.

"This is the parting of our ways," he said. "I can take a good deal, but I won't have my dog called down."

Earl smirked; he knew Santee was jealous. "That's okay with me," he said, and ran through the hammering rain to his car, squeezing the grouse in his arms.

Santee woke before dawn, jammed up against Verna's body heat. He could see the pale mist of breath floating from her nostrils. Icy air flowed through an inch of open window. He slipped out of bed to close it, saw the storm had cleared the weather. Stars glinted like chips of mica in the paling sky, hoarfrost coated the fields and the row of stones along the drive. The puddles in the driveway were frozen solid. It was going to be a cold, unclouded day. He laughed to himself as he got back into the warm bed, wondering what Earl had said when he plucked three partridges that were already cooked.

Two successful hunters, man and dog, return to their truck. (Photograph © Bill Buckley/The Green Agency)

LEARNING TO HUNT

By Jimmy Carter

Jimmy Carter was the thirty-ninth president of the United States, leading the country through the difficult post-Watergate years and presiding over the summit between Egyptian President Anwar Sadat and Israeli Prime Minister Menachem Begin that lead to the historic Camp David Accord. He also ran the country during the Soviet invasion of Afghanistan and subsequent boycott of the 1980 Moscow Olympics, and was the Chief Executive when Iranian student extremists overran the U.S. Embassy in Tehran in 1979, a crisis that contributed greatly to Carter's failure to win re-election in 1980.

That's quite a resumé, and it represents only a small portion—four years, really—in the life of a remarkable man. But throughout all of this, and throughout his life before and after the presidency, Jimmy Carter held the outdoors close to his heart and spent a good deal of time hunting, fishing, and just experiencing the wild world.

Carter also has used his spare time to write. In addition to his many titles of a political nature, he wrote *An Outdoor Journal: Adventures and Reflections*, a warm collection of hunting and fishing reminiscences, where "Learning To Hunt" was first published.

A happy boy with his game. (Photograph courtesy Pennsylvania State Archives, Record Group 31, Department of Commerce, Vacation and Travel Bureau)

Before I was big enough to handle my own gun or even a BB rifle, I was serving proudly as a pickup boy for my father during the frigid hours of the winter dove shoots. Daddy would always call me long before daylight, about 4:30 A.M. sun time. Outside it was remarkably still, except for the roosters, who had often begun to crow. We carried to the truck his guns and a seat made of an empty shotgun-shell box, holding a half case of shells and some lightwood splinters. Sometimes, after ceremonially checking to be sure it was empty, he would let me carry one of the guns.

Our first stop was at a prearranged gathering place, either one of the stores downtown in Plains or perhaps a farmer's house. I'd be filled with a great excitement as we went in to gather around a potbellied stove or a warm hearth fire. Most of the time I was the only child there. There was a feeling of exclusive masculinity within the group when the men talked about hunting and laughed a lot at jokes and ribald accounts of sex adventures that they assumed I could not understand. The men drank big cups of coffee, sometimes laced with spirits, while I was offered a Coca-Cola or perhaps a cup of hot chocolate. It was at such moments that my father was most exalted in my mind.

After a half hour or so, we traveled in as few vehicles as possible to the designated field, where its owner, our host for the morning, described the layout and gave instructions on how to reach the different "stands." With lanterns or flashlights we found our way by the edge of woods, or along a fence, hedgerow, or brush-covered terrace, expecting that some of the latecomers would fill in the less desirable spaces in the center of the open spaces to keep the doves moving if they flew in to light. The fields were relatively small then, because land-breaking and cultivation were done with mules and horses; the large plots of today's tractor cultivation simply did not exist. With shouts and light signals we made sure we were not too close to our neighbors, identified them, and settled down to wait for the first signs of daybreak. If the weather was too cold to bear, Daddy kindled a small fire and trusted me to gather enough sticks around our site to keep it going.

The night was still pitch-black. We could hear the call of owls in the more distant deep woods and then the small killdeers landing and taking off in the field. Later came the sound of crows in the distance and

unseen songbirds among the nearby trees. We were so still that some of them would land almost on top of us. Sometimes the song of a lonely bobwhite quail intimated in its urgent call that it had been separated from the covey and not reunited before last night settled in. Then, as daybreak approached, we would hear the earliest whistle of unseen doves' wings overhead.

After a few minutes the sound of the first shots reverberated across the brightening field, usually around 6:00 A.M., and the dove shoot was underway. The hunters were well within gun range of one another; spent birdshot rained down harmlessly all around us after their skyward trajectory was completed. If anyone grew careless and endangered a neighbor by shooting too low, it was a serious matter indeed, warranting an angry shout of condemnation and a damaged reputation.

Without being told, I learned very early not to comment on Daddy's missed shots, except to phrase a quiet excuse for him. "That one swerved just as you shot, Daddy." "He was pretty far away." "I saw the feathers come out of him." "I think he went down way over yonder in those bushes." "They're sure flying high this morning." I didn't have to do this too often, because Daddy was an experienced hunter and a good marksman; he brought down plenty of doves.

Many years later, after we had returned to Plains from my time in the Navy, I took my own sons hunting. The first time the youngest, Jeffrey, went with me to pick up doves, he didn't know how to protect the sensitivities of his father. During the past two decades I had rarely shot doves and was having a very frustrating morning. Time after time I fired my 20-gauge shotgun, but the doves never wavered in their flight.

Without my noticing, Jeff had picked up the empty shells and carefully arranged them in the dirt.

A couple of my friends walked by us and asked, "How are you doing?"

"Not too well," I replied.

Then Jeffrey spoke up: "Daddy has shot eleven times and ain't hit nothing."

Thanks a lot, son.

When I was a child my main job was to mark where my father's birds fell and to run and pick them up when other birds were not coming in. This assignment wasn't easy if a bird was wounded but still able to run and fly

Parker "DHE" grade 20-gauge shotgun dating from the late 1920s, a gun well suited for hunting mourning doves. (Photograph © William W. Headrick)

short distances. Even those lying still were sometimes indistinguishable in the light-gray frostbitten grass or among empty corn shucks, which looked almost like doves with closed wings. On one memorable occasion, a redtail hawk swooped down just ahead of me and flew up with our dove. Daddy waited until it was safely away from me and then brought down both birds with a long shot. We talked about that for a long time afterwards, with my father cautioning me not to forget that ordinarily hawks do a lot of good and should not be killed. I believe that he felt somewhat guilty about shooting this one, but he never said so.

Even at a great distance, we could identify the other hunters, mostly from their hats. Only a few times in my life did I ever see my father outdoors without a hat, and most of the other men considered themselves partially undressed if they were bareheaded. Headgear became quite distinctive, almost like hallmarks, among the men of our community. This was, of course, before the days of the now ubiquitous and standardized base-

ball caps, whose only distinguishing feature is whether they bear advertisements for farm tractors, bulldozers, fertilizer, pesticides, snuff, or chewing tobacco.

After a couple of hours the shooting became more sporadic; the experienced hunters with the best stands usually had a good mess of doves by then. Most often my father and I were among the first to leave. Daddy wanted to be at his work, and after I was five years old and going to school he had to deliver me to the classroom. These were among my proudest moments: At times I would leave a few feathers casually attached to my jacket or trousers to prove that I had been hunting with my daddy. I don't remember any explanation or excuse ever being offered to the teachers for my tardiness—hunting was a routine part of life in those days.

A little later, Daddy let me use an old single-shot .410 shotgun that he had borrowed from a neighbor, and placed me on the dove field near him. Watching me carefully, he would call out a warning when a dove approached my stand and give me constructive advice

Sporting magazine covers from the thirties and forties, published when Jimmy Carter was a teenager. Owners: Pete Press and Jim Meyer. (Photograph © Howard Lambert)

after I had missed the bird. "You shot too soon." "Lead them a little more." "Let your gun keep on swinging until after you pull the trigger." "Hold your cheek firmly down on the gun stock." "Try to keep both eyes open if you can." I soon began to hit a dove every now and then, with gratifying congratulations from my father.

By the time I was ten years old I had graduated from flips, slingshots, and BB guns to own a .22 caliber Remington pump rifle and a bolt-action 4-shot model .410 shotgun from Sears, Roebuck. I was holding down my own stand on the dove fields, sometimes going with older friends even without Daddy along. And Rachel's husband, Jack Clark, was taking me out hunting every now and then for bobwhite quail, which were plentiful around our house.

We did not call them quail in those days but either "birds" or "pottages" (from the *partridges* of our European forebears). When Daddy said, "I'm going bird hunting," we never thought he meant doves, ducks, turkey, or anything else but quail. We all considered this pursuit to be the ultimate in hunting: The combination of bird dogs, guns, etiquette, the stark beauty of the late-fall and winter woods, the fascinating stories derived from the always unpredictable excursions, the close comradeship among the hunters as they walked along behind the dogs (for safety, Daddy would never shoot with more than one other person at a time), and the delicious quail recipes that were sources of pride within each farm family, all combined to give these experiences a special flavor.

On our farm the production of crops and livestock was paramount, but never incompatible with good hunting. We always had two or three bird dogs, one of them often a puppy that was being trained. We never owned a cat, although some were permitted to live around the barn or outhouses to catch mice and do battle with the large wharf rats which, before Warfarin and D-con, were almost impervious to any existing control methods except a .22 rifle. Our dogs, on the other hand, were considered almost members of the family. They were not babied as personal pets, were never fed so much as to become overweight, and were not allowed by Daddy inside our house. But within those bounds the bird dogs were special, and we let them know it.

Although they were taught to obey orders meticulously, they were not trained in a fancy way. Daddy didn't teach them to "lie down," "sit," "heel," or "stay," because these commands were not considered necessary on the farm. Dogs were shut in a kennel only when a bitch was in heat; otherwise, they ran loose. At a relatively early age they were taught to stop instantly when ordered to "whoa," and to come when they heard "here." "Careful" and "close" were important commands when birds were believed to be nearby, and "Come in here" with a hand signal was used to indicate the side of the trail to be covered next by the dog. Repeated use of the word "dead" kept the dog in the immediate area of a downed bird, and "fetch" was used to have the bird brought to the dog's owner.

Daddy was quite stern with a dog who would not obey, often saying, "If a dog won't mind, he's not worth having." I hate to think of his assessment of my own two bird dogs today; they will point quail but are with me in the coverts too seldom to be well trained. Daddy was gentle, however, with a young dog or one he believed to have made an honest mistake in the field. My father did not believe in the methods described by the sporting magazines for teaching dogs to point in the yard. Ours learned from experience, among the plentiful wild game around our home.

When trained, they were dear to us and had a remarkable monetary value as well. Even during the Depression years on the farm, when cash money was scarce and most trade was by barter or on credit until harvesttime, urban standards applied to the price of good bird dogs. Although Daddy would no more consider selling one of our best dogs than one of

us children, I remember that once he was offered several hundred dollars for a locally renowned liver-spot female pointer—equivalent in some of those poorest crop years to the net annual income from a two-horse farm.

Some of the most disturbing family times were when one of our prized dogs was missing; then my normally calm father grew uncharacteristically distraught. If the dog had gotten lost during a hunt, everyone went to the area to whistle and call until it was found. If we were still unsuccessful before nightfall, Daddy would lay one of his old sweaters or hunting coats on the ground where he had last seen the dog and place a pan of water beside it. In most cases the missing animal would be lying on the garment the next morning. But if one of our dogs just didn't show up by feeding time, the presumption was that it had been sto-

A high compliment indeed for Marble's Knives in this ad from 1938.

len or bitten by a rattlesnake. In most cases, a snakebite was not eventually fatal, and the dog would come home and lie around for a week or two with face or head swollen to more than twice its normal size, often developing a large sore before it finally recovered.

Bird dog theft was the worst threat of all. In our part of the country it was regarded as much worse than stealing horses—almost as bad as kidnapping children. If a stranger showed too much interest in one of our dogs, we would be particularly careful in watching it for a few days. The thief who succeeded could never keep a stolen dog anywhere around its former home, because good dogs were as well known within the community as people and would be recognized immediately if sighted. The general presumption was that some "foreigner" from far-off Albany, Columbus, or Atlanta was guilty.

Daddy was not a superstitious man, but he believed in fortunetellers when it came to finding a lost bird dog—or at least he did not want to overlook the possibility that they might help. There were always a few

around, and he would go from one to the other, following the cryptic advice he received as long as there was any chance. It seemed to me that he and his friends were inclined to remember the successes and forget the failures, so that each time another dog was lost they were hopeful all over again. One time Daddy took me with him to see a large black woman who lived alongside a country road with some brightly painted crescent moons, stars, and an enormous human hand tacked to the trees in front of her house. The lines in the palm of the wooden hand were carefully drawn, with words beside the main ones to signify LIFE, LOVE, PAST, and FUTURE. I remember that she made us wait for a while before she would see us, which was a strange experience in itself for white people in a black woman's yard. When finally my father was invited in, I slipped through the door behind him into the darkened room. The fortuneteller, by her comments, seemed to identify the dog. After asking several questions, she said, "Mr. Earl, you ain't never gonna see that dog ag'in."

He paid her a dollar, and we left. We rode in silence

On point for bobwhite. (Photograph © Stephen Kirkpatrick)

for a while, and then Daddy said, "I expect she's right."

She was.

By the time I was big enough to tote a real shotgun, my use of our dogs was unrestricted, because my father and Jack had carefully trained me on hunting safety, proper manners, and the right way to treat each dog. With my bolt-action .410, I began to hunt by myself with just one dog at a time, usually a close-ranging setter bitch named Lady. One day, about a quarter of a mile east of our house, Lady pointed in a grove of scrub oak trees. I approached carefully, a large covey of quail flushed, and I fired somewhat blindly in the direction of the birds. One fell. This was one of my life's proudest moments. I picked up the quail and ran all the way home.

Daddy was working in the blacksmith shop, where I breathlessly described to him my great adventure. He shared my pride and then looked around and asked me: "Where's your gun?"

I had no idea. When I went back to look, I couldn't find the

A pair of pointers in the field. (Photograph © Bill Buckley/The Green Agency)

place where the covey had flushed. It was especially embarrassing that we had to ask several other people to help before we finally found the shotgun lying among some leaves where I had dropped it. I was thankful that my daddy never mentioned the abandoned gun again, at least to me.

I also hunted squirrels and rabbits by myself, the former with the .22 rifle and the latter with my .410 shotgun. For the first few years I still-hunted for squirrels, sitting quietly in the woods where there was a good stand of oak or hickory trees, or perhaps one of the increasingly rare chestnuts that had survived the blight, and waiting for one of the bushy-tailed creatures to show itself. When he ran or leaped through the trees, I would watch carefully until he stopped. If he saw me, the squirrel would often flatten himself against

the tree trunk or a limb and then move around to keep the tree always between us. I learned to carry with me a long string, which I would tie to a bush. Then I'd move quietly to the other side of the tree, yank the string, and watch for the squirrel to hide from the noisy bush and move into view on my side.

Two or three gray squirrels made a good meal for our family. Fox squirrels were half again as large but not so common, and Daddy told me never to shoot at the flying squirrels, which were too small to eat and somewhat rare. They moved around mostly at night, but every now and then I would see one during daylight hours.

One day Daddy brought me a Boston bulldog puppy, whom I named Bozo. We were inseparable. He turned out to be not only a great pet but also the best

ABOVE: *1930s Browning Automatic 5 shotgun. Owner: Bill Diers. (Photograph © Howard Lambert)*

FACING PAGE: *A North Carolina hunter and his game, 1938. (Photograph courtesy the North Carolina Division of Archives and History)*

squirrel dog in the neighborhood—better than any of the hounds owned by our neighbors. From then on, I walked through the woods with Bozo hunting squirrels. When he treed one, barking furiously, it was a simple matter to get on the other side of the tree and find my quarry.

Bozo became well known among other squirrel hunters in the neighborhood. Early one morning, two of my father's friends came by and borrowed my dog to go hunting. That night, Daddy drove up in his pickup and called me out in the yard. Bozo was lying in the back, dead. He had jumped out of the hunters' car while it was parked in front of a garage in Americus, become confused on the city streets, and been run over by a truck. Mama and Daddy tried to comfort me, but I

didn't want to talk to anyone. I went down in the woods by myself to some places we had hunted together and said some prayers that my dog was safe and happy in heaven. Bozo was the only dog I ever owned as a child, and I kept his picture tacked to the wall of my room until I went off to college.

Rabbits were too plentiful around our fields, house, and garden, providing a lot of good hunting and eating for the people who lived around Archery. The only time I didn't shoot rabbits was while hunting quail. Daddy said if I let the bird dogs run rabbits and I shot them, the dogs would think that was part of their job and it would divert them from their primary responsibility.

This was one rule of my father's that Jack Clark

found fit to ignore when he and I were hunting alone. He shot rabbits even in the presence of our dogs, and they didn't seem to acquire any worse habits. Mama would not cook a rabbit in the summertime—something to do with diet or pests or disease—but they were considered all right when the weather was cold.

Daddy was not a coon hunter and we never owned hound dogs, but on occasion he would go along on a fox hunt—primarily a white man's sport. In our area the fox hunt began by turning the hounds loose at night, then sitting around a campfire and listening to them. There is something special about a fire of any kind, particularly a campfire in the deep woods. Just looking at the colored flames and flickering shadows seems to arouse some instinct from prehistoric times, when gathering around a fire was the source of the clan's comfort and even survival, and where the earliest human conversations were heard on earth. During the leisurely hours of a fox hunt there was plenty of time for silence, a lot of philosophizing, drinking, and the identification and assessment of hounds' voices. The hunters did not expect to catch the foxes, and they knew that a good portion of the next day would have to be spent trying to find all the dogs.

Some of the men were consummate liars, although their tales were always begun in a quiet and unassuming way, as though they were true. Only at the end of a story, or maybe a few minutes afterward, would the listener realize he had been bamboozled.

"The other day I had the damndest experience of my life," one would start. "I was walking along Kinchafoonee Creek down near the Murray place looking for an old sow of mine, and seen a squirrel go out on a little limb that was lying out in the creek. It was kind of in an eddy, and there was a hickory nut caught in a fork of the limb. Just as the squirrel reached down to get the nut, a tremendous bass came up out of the water and swallowed the damn squirrel. I almost fell over backward, and had to sit down and think about what I had seen.

"After about five minutes there was a disturbance in the water, and I saw that bass come up and carefully put another hickory nut in the same place." Long pause. "First time I ever seen a fish squirreling."

* * * *

Hunting coons and possums was a different proposition entirely. It was done for meat, the participants were usually black, and most of the night was spent walking through thick woods and swamps. Even as a young boy I was a sought-after companion when our adult neighbors went hunting for raccoons or opossums, because I was one of the best and most daring tree-climbers around. Mama wouldn't let me stay out all night before a day of school, but at other times I was free to join the hunters.

For that night, three or four men would pool their hound dogs. After the dogs went through a standard ceremony of sniffing and a little snarling and snapping, we were off with a lantern or two, carrying a five-cell flashlight we used only after the dogs had treed an animal. With just a little light from the sky we did without the lanterns in order to save kerosene; it was surprising how well we could see after our eyes became adjusted to the dark. When we hunted on our place, I was familiar with the territory and never got lost, but when we went farther afield it was not easy to know where we were. On clear nights I marked the stars and moon and kept up fairly well with our twists and turns, but in the cloudy or rainy times I had to depend on the others not to get lost. We always hoped that at least one of us hunters knew approximately where we were.

In the woods we walked single file, with enough room between us to keep the bent limbs ahead from springing back to hit the one next in line. But there were other hazards. Busting shins against a log or stump or running into one of the viciously thorned swamp blackberry vines could not be avoided for long. Every now and then we would stop to listen to the dogs; if they weren't hot on a scent we just kept moving along on our own chosen route. One of the men would whoop and holler on occasion so that the dogs would know where we were. Often one of the dogs would check in until it could see us and then disappear again. We all learned to recognize each hound's voice, so that it soon became superfluous to say, "That's old Red," or "Joe's onto somethin'." Still, we never failed to say it anyway.

When the tone or timbre of a dog's baying tightened up, we grew instantly alert and began to move in its direction. The hound's owner went forward and took

Family Traditions (1998) by Scot Storm. (Courtesy Apple Creek Publishing)

charge, encouraging the dog with frequent shouts to move on and also to bay more often, giving us a more uninterrupted description of what was going on. The other dogs, previously scattered through the woods, would then converge on the leading hound. When we got close to the pack of dogs, we squatted down and waited for the finale: the treeing of the raccoon or opossum. There was a lot of guessing (in the form of absolutely positive assertions) about what was being chased, but most of the time it was impossible to be sure. Coons were more inclined toward the deep swamps, while possums preferred the kinds of trees that grow only in more sunshine around the edges of fields or along fences or hedgerows, such as persimmon or black cherry. If the dogs treed in a place for a while and then began another chase, we were pretty certain it was a coon, because coons were more willing and able than possums to leave a tree with a pack of dogs under it.

When we made our final move in to the furiously baying dogs, our path was a straight and fast one through briers, bogs, and streams. Sometimes it was difficult for me to keep up with the excited men. Under the tree, we would turn the beam of the flashlight up and search diligently until we saw the bright reflecting eyes shining back. There were times when we would find two or even three coons or possums in the same tree. They were never shot. Instead, the men would lift me up into the lower branches, I would climb until I reached the right limb and then shake it until the animal fell. If necessary, one of the grown men would help me. On some occasions this process would take more than an hour, but if the dogs' masters were very hungry for fresh meat or if it was almost daybreak, they would shorten the process by cutting down a relatively small and nonmarketable tree to bring their quarry to the ground.

Opossums, on the ground, would usually lie still and pretend to be dead, but the raccoons would back up, face their attackers, and fight until captured. Normally, the coon or possum was soon caught and put into a burlap bag, ideally with minimal injury to all concerned. Then we would induce the excited hounds to begin another chase. But if we made a mistake and let a live bobcat hit the ground, the dogs were in serious trouble. There was a standard joke about the man who climbed a tree and grabbed a bobcat by mistake. After a few minutes of furious scratching and clawing, the man yelled out, "Just shoot up here amongst us—I'd rather take my chances with the bullets!"

Our minimum goal was to catch one animal for each family represented in the hunt, but sometimes luck wasn't with us and some of the men went home empty-handed and disappointed. First

Preparing for a southern duck hunt, circa 1941. (Photograph courtesy Tennessee State Library and Archives)

priority went to whoever owned the dog that struck the trail of the animals we caught. At our house we didn't eat these animals because Mama wouldn't cook them, but I have eaten them many times at other places. It was advisable to keep them caged up for a week or two and fed sweet potatoes or similar vegetables until any remnant of their dubious wild diet was gone. Then one could be sure they were "fitten to eat."

A white family that lived about a half mile from our house had some good hounds and loved to hunt with them. It was also generally known that some pretty good moonshine was produced on their farm; from our front porch we would watch the steady stream of automobiles and pickup trucks visiting there for a few days whenever a new batch had been cooked off. The revenuers caught Mr. Bob fairly regularly, and he was fined and sometimes gone for a few months, but his business seemed to thrive in between these interruptions. He was not condemned by his neighbors. Although Prohibition had been repealed, our state was still dry and there was a good bit of sympathy for a few respectable people who were willing to provide for some of the human needs in the neighborhood, in spite of legal risks to themselves.

Whiskey stills were artfully concealed in the most remote locations, near a stream of good water and where the necessary fire and smoke were screened as thoroughly as possible from any aerial observation. A few times the revenue agents came to notify Daddy that they had discovered a moonshine still on some of his land, and later we would go to the secluded spot and look at the equipment the revenuers had demolished. Sometimes the 'shiners were caught; most of the time they escaped. They devised all kinds of ways to tell that someone had come down a path leading to the still. Then they would abandon the place, or observe it from a distance until it was destroyed or the intruder was identified as an innocent passerby who failed to reappear after a suitable interval.

One night we were coon hunting with a couple of our black neighbors and Mr. Bob when the dogs struck a trail and began to follow it down one of the branches west of his house. We all sat down to listen, but Mr. Bob seemed to become more and more nervous as treeing became imminent. When we finally went to the dogs, they were under a tree right at his moon-

shine still. There was a lot of joking, laughing, and some embarrassment because I was there. We got the coon, and all swore to keep mum about the exact location of its capture. I honored my oath; I didn't even tell my father about it until after I was graduated from college.

Although the Plains area was not on any major flyway, we still had plenty of good duck hunting during the cold winter months. I seldom went to the larger lakes of the Flint and Chattahoochee rivers, which were about fifty miles east and west of our home; even the nearby millponds were not as attractive as the more natural and isolated places. Our swamps, with their remoteness, good cover, and plentiful supply of acorns and other feed, provided an excellent home for the indigenous wood ducks, and during the winter months we would have some scattered flights of migrating teal and mallards come in to stay for a few days. In most of the flat swampy areas, there were a number of permanent "lakes" left where the creek had changed its course, and the eddy or backwater portions of the streams also provided plenty of water for ducks to hide and feed.

We had some favorite places for duck hunting in the swamp lakes and would usually seek them long before dawn, leaving home to go in to shoot during the early morning hours. At other times a friend and I drifted down the larger creeks in a small flat-bottomed plywood boat I built, one of us steering with a few quiet paddle strokes in the stern while the other sat in the bow with the shotgun, ready for startled waterfowl to flush. We didn't get as many ducks while moving down the streams as we did in the swamp lakes, but there was a chance to see much more of the creek wildlife as we traveled long miles through the center of the swamp as silently as possible.

Looking back on my hunting days, it seems obvious that the excitement and challenge of hunting was closely related to the acquisition of food. There was never any question about the morality of hunting, but neither was there any acceptance of killing for the sake of a trophy. Landowners, large and small, thought of wild game as one of the important products of the farm, and studied and applied good conservation practices to enhance the value of this harvest in the proper seasons.

These measures were even confirmed by our religious beliefs. At least once a year in all the churches, the minister offered a sermon on stewardship, in which the responsibilities and joys of landownership were emphasized. Even during the Depression years, when many marginal farm families were on the verge of starvation, their prayers of thanksgiving for the land, streams, and woods were devout and sincere. Often, when I am in a particularly beautiful or isolated place, a vivid image comes to my mind of bowed heads, quiet prayer, and old-fashioned church hymns, as I remember the habits of my youth.

Ducks of all shapes and sizes flutter across a fiery sky. (Photograph © Bill Marchel)

BLIZZARD ON THE RACE TRACK

By Steve Grooms

Steve Grooms has written much about his hunting and fishing adventures around the Midwest, including many articles and stories in *Gray's Sporting Journal*, *Shooting Sportsman*, *Pheasants Forever*, *Gun Dog*, and other sporting magazines. He has also published six books on hunting, fishing, and wildlife, including *Modern Pheasant Hunting* (1982), *Channel Catfish Fever* (1989), and *The Ones That Got Away* (1992).

"Blizzard on the Race Track" appeared in Grooms's 1990 book *Pheasant Hunter's Harvest*.

Circa 1915 English Tad Scott shotgun and shell boxes. Owner: Caribou Gun Club. (Photograph © Howard Lambert)

When I woke up, I didn't know where I was. And, holy cow, what *was* that noise? It sounded like London during the Blitz.

Slowly, consciousness burned away the mists of sleepy confusion. Oh, yeah. I was in a sleeping bag on the floor of a deserted South Dakota farmhouse. Brandy was curled beside me, a paw tucked demurely over her freckled nose. Bill was in the next room. But what was that noise? With each bang, the walls shook and crumbs of plaster trickled down. Glass panes rattled in sloppy window frames in a way that suggested we were in an earthquake. I ventured timidly out of the bag.

The window seemed to have been spray-painted white by vandals in the night. When I found an opening to peer through, I could recognize nothing. Then I understood. We were in a blizzard. The wind howled so maniacally that leafless shrubs strained at their roots. Shelterbelt cottonwoods wrenched side to side like aerobics exercisers. Snow streamed flat across the prairie like something shot from a firehose. Every few seconds, lightning bolts fused earth to sky in a light show from Hell.

Wow. I slid back in the bag, lit a cigar, and found the place marker in my mystery novel. We wouldn't hunt today.

This had been a weird pheasant opener from the start.

Bill and I thought we'd scored a great coup. At a time every motel in South Dakota was booked solid with opening weekend hunters, I was able to rent a cabin at a lakeside resort. Magic words, those: *cabin, lakeside, resort.* We would clean limits of pheasants by the dancing blue waters in front of the cabin, then sit pensively with glasses of whiskey while the setting sun dropped behind the far shoreline in a glory of flame orange.

Ah, but life is full of surprises. The "resort" turned out to be a trailer ghetto full of shabby motor homes. Our "cabin" had not been left unlocked for us, as promised, so we had to roust the proprietor from his bed; he shuffled out in socks and undershorts, reached through the broken window, and opened the door from the inside. The cabin was illuminated by three naked light bulbs dangling from the cardboard ceiling. Coil springs protruded through the plastic upholstery of the furniture. The kitchen tap emitted amber clots of goo in-

stead of water. Throughout the night, burly animals conducted orgies or wars or both inside the cabin walls. Daylight arrived to show us the "lake" was a shallow basin of slimy, blurping algae, almost thick enough to walk upon. I expected at any moment to see some new life form come crawling up out of that primordial ooze.

Our hunting was an extension of the resort experience. The summer had been so wet farmers didn't dare take field machinery into muddy fields to harvest crops. The pheasants were scattered throughout the standing corn where we had no chance of shagging them out. The only rooster we saw taken all day was ground-sluiced by some Alabama boys who never left the comfort of the velour seats in their conversion van to pot the bird. Man, it has to be *loud* to touch off a shot inside a van like that!

That evening Bill and I chewed some rubbery cafe chow mein and discussed our options. "We've got to get out of here," said Bill, with feeling. I agreed. "Out of here and clear away from all this standing corn." We were up early in the morning. We paid up and told the resort man we had to cancel the rest of our reservation. My grandmother had died, poor dear, most unexpectedly.

For three hours we drove south and west on highways lined with discouraging walls of standing corn. Gradually, the land changed, becoming flatter and drier. Corn began sharing the landscape with milo. Farms became bigger, the farm homes more widely dispersed. We had crossed out of the old tallgrass prairie into the Great Plains. "This looks better," I finally said. "More crops down."

Bill studied a map of South Dakota public hunting areas. "Here's a possibility," he said. "It's big, about half a section. Should be a bird out there somewhere. Hang a right in two miles." Soon my red station wagon humped into the corner parking lot of the management area. It was big all right, though more uniform than is ideal. The ground was almost tabletop flat and covered overall with thigh-high wheatgrass. "We might as well start here as anywhere," I said. "It all looks the same."

We had barely closed our guns when Brandy's head snapped down and she bustled northward. Bill and I loped behind. Brandy paused to puzzle out a confusing puddle of scent, then shot away again. Twice her course curved, giving the humans a deeply appreciated

The rump feathers of a rooster ring-necked pheasant. (Photograph © Ron Spomer)

chance to catch up with the galloping springer. Brandy finally did a curling maneuver, staring into the grass with her *"thumb yer safeties"* expression. Bill dropped the rooster that flashed up near him.

"Good shot," I said, panting. "Good dog work," said Bill as he twisted to drop the bird in his game bag. "Uh, speaking of Brandy, where is she?" Brandy was charging through the wheatgrass again, noisily sucking scent. We ran. She ran. The bird ran and ran and ran. About the time Bill and I were ready to give up, Brandy slammed on the brakes and maneuvered cautiously for the flush. Another rooster.

I wheezed as I accepted the fragrant gift from Brandy. Leaning on his Citori, Bill said, "This is crazy. I wonder what Steve Grooms, author of *Modern Pheasant Hunting,* would do in a situation like this." I shook my head. "Bill, I keep saying you've got to develop more cynicism about outdoor writers. They are knaves, fools, and drunks, and the truth is not in them." I added darkly, "Anyway, I've heard stories about that Grooms

character. If he was here he'd be running as stupidly as we've been, only I'm sure he couldn't keep up with us."

"Where's Brandy?"

"She's right . . . uh oh! *Run!*"

The rest is quickly told: two hours, eight chases, six rooster flushes, six shells fired, six retrieves. And every bird ran like a cat with four soup cans tied to his tail. It was the most aerobic pheasant hunt I've known. We had done a 10K marathon in shell vests and boots, toting over-unders. Our shortest chase might have been sixty yards, the longest three times that distance.

Back in the car, Bill drew an arrow on the map toward the management area and carefully penned in the name we'd given it: "The Race Track."

"Jim Layton should have seen this," I said as we drove off in search of a place to sleep. Jim had been our pheasant hunting host in central Iowa for years. A canny pheasant man, Jim was also an incurable optimist. He'd squint at the skies each morning and drawl, "Awww, it

A pheasant makes a run for it across a snowy field. (Photograph © Alan and Sandy Carey)

looks super. I bet them ol' roosters will be settin' real tight today." And he was wrong every time. Every damn time. Whether the skies were gray, blue, or chartreuse with pink polka dots, we never once found Jim's late season Iowa roosters willing to hold tight.

Following a lead from a kind motel lady, Bill and I drove to a farm that might be able to accommodate us. There we met a pleasant middle-aged couple of Dutch descent, their faces etched by years of exposure to prairie weather. He had a farmer's tan. The skin on his neck was as dark as liver while his forehead bore the sickly pale shape of a duck's bill, a negative image of his cap. He called himself a *"dry-land* farmer."

Next to their property was an abandoned farmhouse, a forlorn shell that held silent memories and no furniture. If we didn't mind sleeping on the floor, we were welcome. We weren't told the couple's hospitality would include a visit each morning with fresh-baked chocolate chip cookies and a steaming thermos of coffee.

We spent two happy days camping in the farmhouse. Then the blizzard hit.

I awoke the second time about mid-morning, *Trent's Last Case* folded over my nose like a pup tent. Bill and I peered out the dining room window at an eerie moonscape. My station wagon was a Styrofoam caricature of a car. Every tree seemed to have been sprayed white on its northwest side. Wind buffeted the farmhouse and keened around the gables while the torrent of snow spilled laterally over the prairie.

"We aren't going hunting, are we?" asked Bill. I laughed, "Is that some kind of trick question or something? We'd never even make it out the driveway. The Ford has crummy traction." "Yeah," Bill agreed, "it would be miserable out there, anyway."

I returned to the sleeping bag and Trent. Industrious Bill waterproofed his boots and oiled his Citori.

Minutes later we were both back with noses pressed to the dining room window like kids outside a candy store. "I've been thinking," I said. "Me too," said Bill.

"We'll surely end up in a ditch." "Yeah, but if we don't. . . ." "If we don't, man, it could be *something.*"

We hacked snow off the car with an old broom whose whiskers were all worn off. The snow was almost axle deep. To get on the gravel county road we'd have to punch through a snowy uphill grade. I rocked the car, laying down a track, then floored the accelerator while Bill pushed. With tires whining like poltergeists, the Fairmount slewed left and right, faltered, then popped onto the gravel. We'd take breakfast in town, then attempt to reach The Race Track.

Small town cafes in pheasant country all look pretty much the same, all wonderful, and you feel as much at home in them as you do in your own kitchen. In the front window is a placard cheering on the local football team: "Spear 'em, Spartans!" The breakfast aromas of coffee and bacon and yeasty rolls float amicably over the quiet, steady fragrance of the griddle. On the formica counter, glass cases tempt you with fresh-baked pies and pastries that leak glimmering pools of calories. The menus are plastic with hand-typed inserts, some entrees misspelled. Pale red posters stapled to the walls advertise farm auctions and estate sales, with frequent mentions of "antiques" that you suspect are just old, cheap things that have had a hard life. The paper placemats carry the same improbable wildlife scenes that you've eaten upon since you began habituating such cafes some thirty-five years ago. A kelly green bass with a mouth the size of a garbage can leaps for a dragonfly suspended in a fluorescent orange sky. At one table, large-bodied men guzzle coffee from ivory porcelain mugs and practice the art of understatement. They bang dice in a leather cup on the table to see who gets stuck with the bill, laughing the comfortable laugh of men who have known each other all their lives. And if you are lucky, your waitress will be a silver-haired woman, broad of beam, with smile creases radiating from her eyes. She raised six children and worked the farm with her husband before his first heart attack, when they retired to the Victorian gingerbread home on the edge of town. And you see it in her eyes as she comes around with the coffee: she has spent her life serving food to men as an expression of love. This, for her, is not employment. This, for her, is religion.

The storm had taken down local power lines, so the darkened cafe was jammed with folks clucking about the weather and relishing the novelty of ordering a breakfast that didn't require electricity. We could have coffee, eggs, and pecan rolls but, sorry, no toast. Toast was electric.

At a nearby table, four farmers in bib overalls and seed caps played a game of whist by the shuddering light of a candle. One studied our hunting garb with friendly amusement. He cackled, "Hee, hee, hee! I guess it ain't your day, boys!" I said, "Matter of fact, we think this is our day." He frowned. "You're not hunting pheasants in this weather!" "We're going to give it a try," said Bill. The farmer rolled his eyes. We'd made him a happy man. He had a story to share with everyone he'd meet, and in a small town stories are a more precious currency than folding money.

On the road to The Race Track we passed three vehicles abandoned in crazy postures in the white ditches. Twice we nearly joined them. There were, of course, no other hunters at The Race Track. I seriously doubted there were hunters afoot anywhere in the county that morning.

The blizzard roared relentlessly. To be heard, I had to shout directly in Bill's ear. Just getting out of the car and loading guns was misery. Even Brandy suffered visibly, shivering while we suited up. Bill wore literally every item of clothing he'd brought for the trip, including pajamas, underwear, a two-piece rain suit, and two hats jammed on his head at once. Nothing would have been enough.

About twenty yards from the car, a silver buffaloberry shrub punched through the infinite emptiness of white. It was the only thing I could see that was not snow. I directed Brandy toward it with a flick of my hand. Brandy stuck her head under the shrub, then popped up to stare at me with eyes wide with amazement. There was a little snow cave under the buffaloberry. Brandy slapped the ground twice with both paws. Nothing happened. She ran to the far side of the shrub and popped at the ground again. The rooster was the very picture of misery when he crawled out. He squatted and flushed the only direction he could fly, straight down the wind. Bill's shot tumbled him.

The next moment is one of my favorite memories of Brandy. After a decade of hunting pheasants in her own way, she totally reinvented the sport. One rooster

Hunting pheasant on the prairie. (Photograph © Ron Spomer)

sufficed to teach Brandy the novel reality of this situation. She rose on her hind legs, forepaws dangling like a Kodiak bear. Straining to make herself tall, Brandy peered around for another bush. There was one fifty yards to the west. Brandy plowed straight to it, not using her nose, not quartering, and jammed her head under the shrub. That one held a hen. Then Brandy lifted, bear-like, scanning for another shrub.

Each time she rooted under a bush, Bill and I arranged ourselves downwind for a shot. The shooting was not as easy as it must sound. We couldn't hear the flushes, and to look upwind toward Brandy was pain-

ful. Twice roosters rocketed by us so quickly our frozen hands couldn't react fast enough. A pair of roosters escaped when I peeped upwind too long and got both eyes packed with snow like a vaudeville clown catching a cream pie in his face.

In between bushes we walked backwards with arms wrapped around our guns, gloved hands clamped up under our armpits, looking like two of Napoleon's musketmen in retreat from Moscow. Icicles hung from our moustaches. We could only walk with our backs to the wind, and standing upright was impossible. If we leaned back into it, strong hands of Canadian air supported us at improbable angles. When I had to get rid of my breakfast coffee I was sorely tempted just to let fly down my leg. It would be so warm . . . for a while, anyway.

Some birds refused to fly until Brandy cuffed them around. Once Brandy burrowed out of sight under the snow along a fence. We could trace her progress under the white drifts by the hummocky trail she made, like a mole's runway. She emerged at last with a crippled rooster in her jaws. "He wouldn't have made it through the next night anyway," Bill said. Four times Brandy returned to us with hens, unhurt, in her mouth. From under some buckbrush, Brandy routed out a rooster that zipped past me like a bolt from a crossbow. I turned to take him as a straightaway. That made five in the bag, one to go.

We were walking crablike, sideways to the wind, when I called to Bill. Brandy sat whining on the high gravel road that divided two parts of the management area. The frozen road was so cold she lifted one paw then the other from it. "Brandy wants us to cross," I yelled. Doing that would expose us to the worst of the wind while we negotiated two tricky barbed wire fences. Bill roared in my ear, "Whatever Brandy wants today, she gets!"

As Bill crossed the fence, he came down on top of a hen. Seconds later we heard the harsh metallic two-note rasp of a rooster. A large cock with a broken wing

sprinted from a clump of weedy trash, looking impossibly bright like molten copper against the white. Brandy hit him in a tumbling flurry of snow. We were done.

"I don't believe it," said Bill, shaking his two hats. "One thing," I said, "I wish Jim had been here to see this." "Yeah," Bill agreed. "It finally happened. Them ol' roosters were settin' real tight."

The return to the car was an almost pleasant downwind jaunt. I forgot to put Brandy on heel and only remembered when she waded into the ditch to claw at another buffaloberry bush. After slapping her paws several times, Brandy picked up the rooster that refused to flush. We released him into the whirling oblivion of white, praying he'd soon find a haven somewhere downwind.

A dainty A. H. Fox 20-gauge shotgun, circa 1918. (Photograph © William W. Headrick)

'BESS' STORY

By John Madson

Labrador retrievers were not widely available as hunting dogs in this country when the twentieth century began; in fact, the dog that is now the most popular dog in America did not arrive here in serious numbers until the twenties and thirties. But today the Lab is considered the quintessential retriever, a dog now deeply intertwined with the hunting tradition in this country and a representation of all that is right about the pursuit of game.

The pursuit of game was a passion of the late John Madson. The author wrote stories for national magazines such as *Smithsonian*, *Audubon*, and *National Geographic*, and published many books about the outdoors, including *Stories from under the Sky* (1961), *Out Home* (1979), *Where the Sky Began: The Land of the Tallgrass Prairie* (1982), and *Up on the River* (1985). He died in 1995, the year "Bess' Story" first appeared in print.

A frosty-headed Lab in flooded timber. (Photograph © Bill Buckley / The Green Agency)

Larry Reid stopped by awhile back, as he often does when he's got a new duck call. A new old one, I mean. He's afflicted with galloping collectivitis for vintage wildfowl calls, which isn't a bad way to go considering that they tend to appreciate in value, take up less room than a decoy collection, and never need dusting. Wives notice things like that—and a duck hunter can do with all the wifely goodwill he can get.

Settling down in my boar's nest of an office, Larry led me through the labyrinth of events that had resulted in his most recent acquisition—a battered walnut tube that was highballing mallards when Harding was president. The account of this odyssey lasted nearly as long as Harding's term of office.

At last the yarn was spun, the antique duck call slathered with praise, and a reflective pause entered the proceedings.

"Reid," I observed, "for you, duck hunting is just an excuse to hunt junker duck calls."

"That is base calumny," he replied stiffly. "There's nothing I'd rather hunt than ducks. Especially when there's a bonus."

"Like another old duck call?

"No, better than that . . ."

And away he went, again.

When things are right, the Batchtown Flats are a glory hole. A broad embayment of the Mississippi behind the Winfield Dam in southwestern Illinois, it's a thousand-acre duck haven of smartweed, millet, mudflats, and open shallows.

On that November day, though, things were not right. Comes to that, things couldn't have been much worse. Bluebird weather—clear, warm, quiet. The kind of day when Batchtown hunters have been known to fish for crappies from their blinds. At the Batchtown check station, there had been a wishful rumor that a new flight of ducks was on its way—but no one put much stock in that. Not with the forecast of a day in the balmy 60s with no weather fronts up north to push anything southward.

But you go hunting when you can, and Larry and his gunning partner, veterinarian Art Lippoldt, figured that hanging around a duck marsh beats hanging around town. Which, of course, it always does.

And so they headed out to their blind on Turner Island, a maze of shallow sloughs and marshy potholes in the middle of the Mississippi, a half-mile west of the Batchtown Flats. Not once in the two-mile run to the island had there been any sign of ducks. The big island had seen a lot of red-letter days in the past, but this wasn't one of them. Not at first, anyway. "Which just goes to prove," Larry said, "that you never know about duck hunting."

He and Doc set their spread of 75 decoys and sat back with pipes and coffee, contemplating smartweed beds and quiet waters that remained steadfastly duckless.

Doc had his female black Lab, Windy, as usual. They came as a set. Larry had his black Lab, Bess—one of Windy's pups from six years earlier. Bess was swollen and miserable with a false pregnancy of the sort she often had after a heat period, but Doc assured Larry that the condition wasn't harmful, just uncomfortable. "I almost left Bess at home that day," Larry said, "but she sweet-talked me out of it. She wanted to go hunting so bad."

Full sunup, and still no sign of ducks anywhere in the sky. Then, Larry remembers, "The flats seemed to explode."

The eastern sky suddenly was skeined with ducks, newcomers that began working the decoy spreads in spite of the guns. Poultry all over the place—but not over Turner Island. There, peace and serenity reigned under a blue and empty sky.

Still, you hang around, never knowing when a few scraps might fall off the table. From out of nowhere, a lone mallard drake swung over the decoys in easy range. Larry took the shot, and Bess hit the water to fetch the day's first duck.

An hour later, two drake mallards and a hen came in off the river, answered the calls, and set their wings. Larry and Doc each dropped a greenhead, the birds were neatly retrieved, and tranquility again settled over their blind. Off to the east, it still sounded like a Juarez election. Through Doc's binoculars, flight after flight of ducks could be seen settling into the flats while our

Parker "VH" grade waterfowling shotgun, circa 1924, Mason "Glass-Eye" grade duck decoys, and a graceful Canada goose decoy carved by the famous artisan Charles Birch in the mid-twenties. (Photograph © William W. Headrick)

A hunter carrying a decoy bag in a half-frozen river. (Photograph © Bill Buckley/The Green Agency)

ABOVE: *Single mallard in flight. (Photograph © Bill Marchel)*

FACING PAGE: *Labrador and decoys: a classic hunting scene. (Photograph © William H. Mullins)*

two heroes languished with cold guns and dry dogs. Slow torture of the worst kind, sitting under an empty sky while a hundred other guys were having powder fits less than a mile away.

It was more than any duck hunter could endure. Something had to be done even if it was wrong. In late morning Doc said, "Some of those guys are bound to have killed out by now. One of us should go back to the check station and see if we can get a blind over there in Hog Heaven . . ."

Doc won the toss, and Larry made the run to the landing alone. When he drove his pickup into the check station's parking lot, one look at the traffic told him the trip had been for nothing. As the flights of new ducks had come pouring in, the word had gone out and local hunters were waiting to take over hot blinds where limits had been filled. Larry joined the crowd, but at almost noon he was still twelfth on the list.

Enough of that. "Take my name off the list," he told the officer in charge. "I'd rather be out there on Turner Island taking my chances than messing around here."

He took his time going back. Why hurry? There were ducks throughout the flats—but still none in sight around the island. He hid the boat and walked over to the blind where Doc was grinning the big hello.

"What are you so happy about?" Larry growled.

"Before I let you in," said Doc, "you have to guess what's in the blind that wasn't here when you left."

"Okay. So how many did you kill?"

"I got three blacks," Doc replied

"What? I'm back there sweating out a line while you're sacking some black mallards?"

"Who said anything about ducks? Look at this."

On the floor of the blind lay Larry's Bess, with three black puppies no bigger than dressed teal. Soon

From a Blind *(1953) by Richard E. Bishop. (Courtesy of Aaron Ashley, Inc.)*

after Larry had left, Bess had begun scratching under the seat of the blind—and once she began whelping, she made steady progress.

"She's had two of 'em within the last half hour," Doc explained proudly. "No problems, though. When you told me about her false pregnancy, I didn't pay much attention. This would have made the fourth time in the last two years, right?"

Right—except that Larry suddenly remembered the summer weekend when he'd attended a drawing for blind sites. Some of the hunters had brought their dogs and one big male Lab, in particular, had seemed smitten with Bess. A-huh . . .

"What are we going to do?" Larry asked.

"Just let nature take its course," Doc replied, "and keep hoping for ducks. No sense moving her and the pups as long as everything keeps going as it has so far."

At that point, a lone drake almost knocked their caps off. Doc dropped the greenhead just beyond the decoys, a cripple. "Grab your dog!" he said. "We don't want Bess to get wet!"

Larry seized a black neck with one hand and

opened the door to the dog ramp with the other. Off and away went the Lab, with a surging splash.

"Reid!" yelled Doc. "You've got hold of Windy! That's Bess after that duck!"

No whistling or yelling could turn the gallant Bess. Lunging through the shallows, spraying mud and water widely, she finally caught the mallard when it became tangled in heavy smartweeds 75 yards from the blind. Bird in mouth, she trudged heavily back to a warm welcome.

Doc was bent on keeping the pups as warm and dry as possible. A perfect solution was at hand. Three of the mallard drakes and an old towel were arranged on the roof of the blind to form a nest in the warm sun and dry willow branches. It's doubtful that any swamp dogs, anywhere or anytime, ever had a more suitable welcome to the special world that would honor them and which, hopefully, they would honor in turn.

"They nestled into those greenheads as if they were trying to retrieve them," Larry said. "And about then, pup number four arrived . . ."

So did more mallards—a christening gift from the Red Gods, some old hunters might say. As if drawn by the mewing puppies, ducks began coming out of the clear November sky in singles, pairs, small bunches. For the next hour or so, there was no thought of anything back in town, and the most important family problems were those being presented by Lady Bess. The dog chute had to be carefully guarded and blocked, for every time the hunters sounded their calls, Bess would be up and ready to go. As a fifth greenhead was added to the bag, a fifth puppy was added to the little nest on the blind's roof. Soon there was a sixth puppy. The nest was being rapidly outgrown, but the wherewithal to enlarge it continued to drop out of the sky.

"This has to be some kind of record," Larry said as he moved puppies down into the blind to nurse.

"How so?" Doc asked.

"You ever heard of anyone hunting ducks with eight Labrador retrievers?"

The rest of the hunt was a happy confusion of filling limits and tending a half-dozen squirming objects that were as black and shiny as lumps of anthracite. With 10 drake mallards and six puppies, the hunters decided to call it a day, pick up, and report to the check station.

That establishment was basking in the sweet, smoky ambience that check stations always seem to have when the Brotherhood of the Drippy Nose has limited out. Grinning hunters with heavy strings of mallards and pintails stood about, still sharing the common adventure and the many marvels of the day. There was far more talking than listening.

With carefully calculated nonchalance, Larry laid out 10 mallards on the checking table.

"Looks like you guys did the right thing, going back to Turner," said the biologist in charge.

"You know it!" Doc broke in. "How about that? Ten greenheads and six blacks . . ."

"Six blacks? Are you crazy? That puts you guys way over the limit!"

"No limit on this kind of blacks," Doc grinned, and began hauling puppies out of the pockets of his big hunting coat. That shut off every other conversation in the room. It was the hit of the show, being played stage center to an audience of stern critics—all of whom gave rave reviews. Half the puppies were spoken for on the spot. After all, blood will tell—and how can any retriever whelped in a duck blind turn out to be anything but a top dog?

Out in the truck, Bess added pup number seven to the Lab population. An eighth and last puppy would arrive at home.

Larry settled back in his chair, I poured more coffee, and we both reflected in the warm afterglow of a well-told tale.

"A hunt to remember," I offered.

"Deed it was," said Larry. "Sure, Doc and I both remember when there were more ducks moving ahead of a northern front, or other hunts with odd twists of luck. Some mighty interesting dogwork, too."

"But I've never seen anything to match Bess' performance that day. It's been over 20 years, but I still remember every detail. The way I figure it, the best duck hunts come in three parts: planning, doing, and remembering. I can't say which part is the best. Can you?"

No, I can't.

But if there's anything better than a perfect three-part hunt and eight new Labs, well, Larry and I will keep our mouths shut while you tell us about it.

PERMISSIONS

We have made every effort to determine original sources and locate copyright holders of the excerpts in this book. Grateful acknowledgment is made to the writers, publishers, and agencies listed below for permission to reprint material copyrighted or controlled by them. Please bring to our attention any errors of fact, omission, or copyright.

"Remembering Shooting-Flying: A Key West Letter" by Ernest Hemingway, from *By-Line: Ernest Hemingway,* edited by William White. Copyright © 1935 by Ernest Hemingway. Copyright renewed © 1963 by Mary Hemingway. Copyright © 1967 by Mary Hemingway. Reprinted by permission of Scribner, a Division of Simon & Schuster, Inc.

"Why I Taught My Boys To Be Hunters" from *An American Hunter* by Archibald Rutledge. Copyright © 1937 by the Frederick A. Stokes Company. Reprinted by permission of Jim Casada.

"Pa'tridge Fever—Cause and Cure" by Gordon MacQuarrie. Copyright © 1941 by Gordon MacQuarrie. Reprinted by permission of Ellen Gibson Wilson.

"Shift of the Wind" by Sigurd F. Olson. Copyright © 1944 by Sigurd F. Olson. Reprinted by permission of Robert K. Olson.

"November Was Always the Best" from *The Old Man and the Boy* by Robert Ruark. Copyright © 1953, 1954 by Robert Ruark, copyright © 1955–1957 by Robert Ruark. Copyright © 1985 by Harold Matson, Paul Gitlin, and Chemical Bank. Reprinted by permission of Henry Holt and Company, LLC.

"Jake's Rangers Hunt the Whitetail" from *Upriver and Down: Stories from the Maine Woods* by Edmund Ware Smith. Copyright © 1965 by Edmund Ware Smith. Copyright renewed © 1993 by Mary Smith. Reprinted by permission of Brandt & Brandt Literary Agents, Inc.

"Brown Bear the Hard Way" by Bob Brister. Copyright © 1971 by Bob Brister. Reprinted by permission of the author.

"Share and Share Alike" from *Never Sniff a Gift Fish* by Patrick F. McManus. Copyright © 1979, 1980, 1981, 1982, 1983 by Patrick F. McManus. Reprinted by permission of Henry Holt and Company, LLC.

"The Unclouded Day" from *Heart Songs and Other Stories* by E. Annie Proulx. Copyright © 1985, 1988 by E. Annie Proulx. Reprinted by permission of Scribner, a Division of Simon & Schuster, Inc.

"Learning To Hunt" from *An Outdoor Journal* by Jimmy Carter. Copyright © 1988, 1994 by Jimmy Carter. Reprinted by permission of the University of Arkansas Press.

"Blizzard on the Race Track" from *Pheasant Hunter's Harvest* by Steve Grooms. Copyright © 1990 by Steve Grooms. Reprinted by permission of The Lyons Press.

"Bess' Story" by John Madson. Copyright © 1995 by John Madson. Reprinted by permission of Dycie Madson.